DOVER·THRIFT·EDITIONS

Poems and Songs

ROBERT BURNS

DOVER PUBLICATIONS, INC.
New York

Note

ROBERT BURNS (1759–1796), the national poet of Scotland, immeasurably enriched English literature as a whole with his unforgettable works. The 43 poems in the present new anthology include: fifteen major pieces from the three editions of *Poems, Chiefly in the Scottish Dialect* that were issued during Burns's lifetime (1786, 1787 and 1793; the works chosen are representative of his satirical, contemplative, epistolary, sentimental, narrative and purely lyrical veins, both in Lowlands Scots and in standard English); the posthumous satirical piece "Holy Willie's Prayer"; twenty-five texts for songs (all written to fit traditional tunes) contributed by Burns to two multivolume publications that continued long after his death, James Johnson's *Scots Musical Museum* (1787–1803) and George Thomson's *Select Collection of Original Scottish Airs for the Voice* (1793–1818; these song texts, sometimes partially based on preexisting lyrics to the songs in question, are possibly Burns's most widely known works—one need only mention "Auld Lang Syne" and "Comin thro' the Rye"); and two post-humously published song texts, one of them the irreverently auto-biographical "There Was a Lad."

DOVER THRIFT EDITIONS
EDITOR: STANLEY APPELBAUM

Copyright © 1991 by Dover Publications, Inc.
All rights reserved under Pan American and International
Copyright Conventions.

Published in Canada by General Publishing Company, Ltd.,
30 Lesmill Road, Don Mills, Toronto, Ontario.
Published in the United Kingdom by Constable and Company, Ltd.,
3 The Lanchesters, 162–164 Fulham Palace Road, London W6 9ER.

This new anthology, first published by Dover Publications, Inc., in 1991, contains 43 poems reprinted from *The Complete Poetical Works of Robert Burns, Cambridge Edition*, Houghton Mifflin Company, Boston (The Riverside Press, Cambridge), in 1897. The table of contents, glossary and alphabetical lists of titles and of first lines are adapted from the corresponding sections of the 1897 volume. The Note above has been written specially for the present Dover edition.

Manufactured in the United States of America
Dover Publications, Inc.,
31 East 2nd Street, Mineola, N.Y. 11501

Library of Congress Cataloging-in-Publication Data

Burns, Robert, 1759–1796.
[Poems.   Selections]
Poems and songs / Robert Burns.
p.   cm. — (Dover thrift editions)
"Contains 43 poems reprinted from the Complete poetical works of
Robert Burns, Cambridge edition, Houghton Mifflin Company, Boston
(The Riverside Press, Cambridge), in 1897" — Copr. p.
Includes bibliographical references and index.
ISBN 0-486-26863-2 (pbk.)
I. Title.   II. Series.
PR4303   1991
821'.6 — dc20   91-14152
                                            CIP

Contents

iii

SONGS FROM JOHNSON'S *SCOTS MUSICAL MUSEUM* (1787–1803)

AND THOMSON'S *SCOTTISH AIRS* (1793–1818)

MISCELLANEOUS SONGS

The Twa Dogs

A TALE

'T was in that place o' Scotland's isle
That bears the name of auld King Coil,
Upon a bonie day in June,
When wearing thro' the afternoon,
Twa dogs, that were na thrang at hame,
Forgathered ance upon a time.

The first I 'll name, they ca'd him Cæsar,
Was keepit for "his Honor's" pleasure:
His hair, his size, his mouth, his lugs,
Shew'd he was nane o' Scotland's dogs;
But whalpit some place far abroad,
Whare sailors gang to fish for cod.

His lockèd, letter'd, braw brass collar
Shew'd him the gentleman an' scholar;
But tho' he was o' high degree,
The fient a pride, nae pride had he;
But wad hae spent an hour caressin,
Ev'n wi' a tinkler-gipsy's messin;
At kirk or market, mill or smiddie,
Nae tawted tyke, tho' e'er sae duddie,
But he wad stan't, as glad to see him,
An' stroan't on stanes an' hillocks wi' him.

The tither was a ploughman's collie,
A rhyming, ranting, raving billie,
Wha for his friend an' comrade had him,
And in his freaks had Luath ca'd him,
After some dog in Highland sang,
Was made lang syne—Lord knows how lang.

He was a gash an' faithfu' tyke,
As ever lap a sheugh or dyke.
His honest, sonsie, baws'nt face
Ay gat him friends in ilka place;
His breast was white, his tousie back

1

Weel clad wi' coat o' glossy black;
His gawsie tail, wi' upward curl,
Hung owre his hurdies wi' a swirl.

Nae doubt but they were fain o' ither,
And unco pack an' thick thegither;
Wi' social nose whyles snuff'd an' snowkit;
Whyles mice an' moudieworts they howkit;
Whyles scour'd awa' in lang excursion,
An' worry'd ither in diversion;
Till tir'd at last wi' monie a farce,
They sat them down upon their arse,
An' there began a lang digression
About the "lords o' the creation."

CÆSAR

I 've aften wonder'd, honest Luath,
What sort o' life poor dogs like you have;
An' when the gentry's life I saw,
What way poor bodies liv'd ava.

Our laird gets in his rackèd rents,
His coals, his kain, an' a' his stents:
He rises when he likes himsel;
His flunkies answer at the bell;
He ca's his coach; he ca's his horse;
He draws a bonie silken purse,
As lang 's my tail, whare, thro' the steeks,
The yellow letter'd Geordie keeks.

Frae morn to e'en it's nought but toiling,
At baking, roasting, frying, boiling;
An' tho' the gentry first are stechin,
Yet ev'n the ha' folk fill their pechan
Wi' sauce, ragouts, an sic like trashtrie,
That's little short o' downright wastrie:
Our whipper-in, wee, blastit wonner,
Poor, worthless elf, it eats a dinner,
Better than onie tenant-man
His Honor has in a' the lan';
An' what poor cot-folk pit their painch in,
I own it 's past my comprehension.

LUATH

Trowth, Cæsar, whyles they 're fash't eneugh:
A cotter howkin in a sheugh,
Wi' dirty stanes biggin a dyke,
Baring a quarry, an' sic like;
Himsel, a wife, he thus sustains,
A smytrie o' wee duddie weans,
An' nought but his han' darg to keep
Them right an' tight in thack an' rape.

An' when they meet wi' sair disasters,
Like loss o' health or want o' masters,
Ye maist wad think, a wee touch langer,
An' they maun starve o' cauld and hunger:
But how it comes, I never kend yet,
They 're maistly wonderfu' contented;
An' buirdly chiels, an' clever hizzies,
Are bred in sic a way as this is.

CÆSAR

But then to see how ye 're negleckit,
How huff'd, an' cuff'd, an' disrespeckit!
Lord, man, our gentry care as little
For delvers, ditchers, an' sic cattle;
They gang as saucy by poor folk,
As I wad by a stinking brock.

I 've notic'd, on our laird's court-day,
(An' monie a time my heart 's been wae),
Poor tenant bodies, scant o' cash,
How they maun thole a factor's snash:
He 'll stamp an' threaten, curse an' swear
He 'll apprehend them, poind their gear;
While they maun staun', wi' aspect humble,
An' hear it a', an' fear an' tremble!

I see how folk live that hae riches;
But surely poor-folk maun be wretches!

LUATH

They 're nae sae wretched 's ane wad think:
Tho' constantly on poortith's brink,
They 're sae accustom'd wi' the sight,
The view o't gies them little fright.

Then chance an' fortune are sae guided,
They 're ay in less or mair provided;
An' tho' fatigu'd wi' close employment,
A blink o' rest 's a sweet enjoyment.

The dearest comfort o' their lives,
Their grushie weans an' faithfu' wives;
The prattling things are just their pride,
That sweetens a' their fire-side.

An' whyles twalpennie worth o' nappy
Can mak the bodies unco happy:
They lay aside their private cares,
To mind the Kirk and State affairs;
They 'll talk o' patronage an' priests,
Wi' kindling fury i' their breasts,
Or tell what new taxation 's comin,
An' ferlie at the folk in Lon'on.

As bleak-fac'd Hallowmass returns,
They get the jovial, ranting kirns,
When rural life, of ev'ry station,
Unite in common recreation;
Love blinks, Wit slaps, an' social Mirth
Forgets there's Care upo' the earth.

That merry day the year begins,
They bar the door on frosty win's;
The nappy reeks wi' mantling ream,
An' sheds a heart-inspiring steam;
The luntin pipe, an' sneeshin mill,
Are handed round wi' right guid will;
The cantie auld folks crackin crouse,
The young anes ranting thro' the house—
My heart has been sae fain to see them,
That I for joy hae barkit wi' them.

Still it 's owre true that ye hae said
Sic game is now owre aften play'd;
There's monie a creditable stock
O' decent, honest, fawsont folk,
Are riven out baith root an' branch,
Some rascal's pridefu' greed to quench,
Wha thinks to knit himsel the faster
In favor wi' some gentle master,
Wha, aiblins thrang a parliamentin',
For Britain's guid his saul indentin'—

CÆSAR

Haith, lad, ye little ken about it:
For Britain's guid! guid faith! I doubt it.
Say rather, gaun as Premiers lead him—:
An' saying aye or no 's they bid him:
At operas an' plays parading,
Mortgaging, gambling, masquerading:
Or maybe, in a frolic daft,
To Hague or Calais taks a waft,
To mak a tour an' tak a whirl,
To learn *bon ton*, an' see the worl'.

There, at Vienna or Versailles,
He rives his father's auld entails;
Or by Madrid he taks the rout,
To thrum guitars an' fecht wi' nowt;
Or down Italian vista startles,
Whore-hunting amang groves o' myrtles
Then bowses drumlie German-water,
To mak himsel look fair an' fatter,
An' clear the consequential sorrows,
Love-gifts of Carnival signoras.

For Britain's guid! for her destruction!
Wi' dissipation, feud an' faction.

LUATH

Hech, man! dear sirs! is that the gate
They waste sae monie a braw estate!
Are we sae foughten an' harass'd
For gear ta gang that gate at last?

O would they stay aback frae courts,
An' please themsels wi' countra sports,
It wad for ev'ry ane be better,
The laird, the tenant, an' the cotter!
For thae frank, rantin, ramblin billies,
Fient haet o' them 's ill-hearted fellows:
Except for breakin o' their timmer,
Or speakin lightly o' their limmer,
Or shootin of a hare or moor-cock,
The ne'er-a-bit they 're ill to poor folk.

But will ye tell me, master Cæsar:
Sure great folk's life 's a life o' pleasure?
Nae cauld nor hunger e'er can steer them,
The vera thought o't need na fear them.

CÆSAR

Lord, man, were ye but whyles whare I am,
The gentles, ye wad ne'er envý 'em!

It 's true, they need na starve or sweat,
Thro' winter's cauld, or simmer's heat;
They 've nae sair wark to craze their banes,
An' fill auld-age wi' grips an' granes:
But human bodies are sic fools,
For a' their colleges an' schools,
That when nae real ills perplex them,
They mak enow themsels to vex them;
An' ay the less they hae to sturt them,
In like proportion, less will hurt them.

A countra fellow at the pleugh,
His acre 's till'd, he 's right eneugh;
A countra girl at her wheel,
Her dizzen 's done, she 's unco weel;
But gentlemen, an' ladies warst,
Wi' ev'n down want o' wark are curst:
They loiter, lounging, lank an' lazy;
Tho' deil-haet ails them, yet uneasy:
Their days insipid, dull an' tasteless;
Their nights unquiet, lang an' restless.

An' ev'n their sports, their balls an' races,
Their galloping through public places,
There 's sic parade, sic pomp an' art,
The joy can scarcely reach the heart.

The men cast out in party-matches,
Then sowther a' in deep debauches;
Ae night they 're mad wi' drink an' whoring,
Niest day their life is past enduring.

The ladies arm-in-arm in clusters,
As great an' gracious a' as sisters;
But hear their absent thoughts o' ither,
They 're a' run deils an' jads thegither.
Whyles, owre the wee bit cup an' platie,
They sip the scandal-potion pretty;
Or lee-lang nights, wi' crabbit leuks
Pore owre the devil's pictur'd beuks;
Stake on a chance a farmer's stackyard,
An' cheat like onie unhang'd blackguard.

There 's some exceptions, man an' woman;
But this is Gentry's life in common.

By this, the sun was out o' sight,
An' darker gloamin brought the night;
The bum-clock humm'd wi' lazy drone;
The kye stood rowtin i' the loan;
When up they gat, an' shook their lugs,
Rejoic'd they were na *men*, but *dogs*;
An' each took aff his several way,
Resolv'd to meet some ither day.

Scotch Drink

Gie him strong drink until he wink,
    That 's sinking in despair;
An' liquor guid to fire his bluid,
    That 's prest wi' grief an' care:
There let him bowse, and deep carouse,
    Wi' bumpers flowing o'er,
Till he forgets his loves or debts,
    An' minds his griefs no more.
                    SOLOMON'S PROVERBS, xxxi. 6, 7.

I

Let other poets raise a fracas
'Bout vines, an' wines, an' drucken Bacchus,
An' crabbit names an' stories wrack us,
　　　　An' grate our lug:
I sing the juice Scotch bear can mak us,
　　　　In glass or jug.

II

O thou, my Muse! guid auld Scotch drink!
Whether thro' wimplin worms thou jink,
Or, richly brown, ream owre the brink,
　　　　In glorious faem,
Inspire me, till I lisp an' wink,
　　　　To sing thy name!

III

Let husky wheat the haughs adorn,
An' aits set up their awnie horn,
An' pease an' beans, at e'en or morn,
　　　　Perfume the plain:
Leeze me on thee, John Barleycorn,
　　　　Thou king o' grain!

IV

On thee aft Scotland chows her cood,
In souple scones, the wale o' food!
Or tumbling in the boiling flood
　　　　Wi' kail an' beef;
But when thou pours thy strong heart's blood,
　　　　There thou shines chief.

V

Food fills the wame, an' keeps us livin;
Tho' life 's a gift no worth receivin,
When heavy-dragg'd wi' pine an' grievin;
　　　　But oil'd by thee,
The wheels o' life gae down-hill, scrievin,
　　　　Wi' rattlin glee.

VI

Thou clears the head o' doited Lear,
Thou cheers the heart o' drooping Care;
Thou strings the nerves o' Labor sair,
   At 's weary toil;
Thou ev'n brightens dark Despair
    Wi' gloomy smile.

VII

Aft, clad in massy siller weed,
Wi' gentles thou erects thy head;
Yet, humbly kind in time o' need,
    The poor man's wine:
His wee drap parritch, or his bread,
    Thou kitchens fine.

VIII

Thou art the life o' public haunts:
But thee, what were our fairs and rants?
Ev'n godly meetings o' the saunts,
    By thee inspir'd,
When, gaping, they besiege the tents,
    Are doubly fir'd.

IX

That merry night we get the corn in,
O sweetly, then, thou reams the horn in!
Or reekin on a New-Year mornin
    In cog or bicker,
An' just a wee drap sp'ritual burn in,
    An' gusty sucker!

X

When Vulcan gies his bellows breath,
An' ploughmen gather wi' their graith,
O rare! to see thee fizz an' freath
    I' th' lugget caup!
Then Burnewin comes on like death
    At ev'ry chaup.

XI

Nae mercy, then, for airn or steel:
The brawnie, bainie, ploughman chiel,
Brings hard owrehip, wi' sturdy wheel,
      The strong forehammer,
Till block an' studdie ring an' reel,
      Wi' dinsome clamour.

XII

When skirlin weanies see the light,
Thou maks the gossips clatter bright,
How fumbling cuifs their dearies slight;
      Wae worth the name!
Nae howdie gets a social night,
      Or plack frae them.

XIII

When neebors anger at a plea,
An' just as wud as wud can be,
How easy can the barley-brie
      Cement the quarrel!
It 's aye the cheapest lawyer's fee,
      To taste the barrel.

XIV

Alake! that e'er my Muse has reason,
To wyte her countrymen wi' treason!
But monie daily weet their weason
      Wi' liquors nice,
An' hardly, in a winter season,
      E'er spier her price.

XV

Wae worth that brandy, burnin trash!
Fell source o' monie a pain an' brash!
Twins monie a poor, doylt, drucken hash,
      O' half his days;
An' sends, beside, auld Scotland's cash
      To her warst faes.

XVI

Ye Scots, wha wish auld Scotland well!
Ye chief, to you my tale I tell,
Poor, plackless devils like mysel!
       It sets you ill,
Wi' bitter, dearthfu' wines to mell,
       Or foreign gill.

XVII

May gravels round his blather wrench,
An' gouts torment him, inch by inch,
Wha twists his gruntle wi' a glunch
       O' sour disdain,
Out owre a glass o' whisky-punch
       Wi' honest men!

XVIII

O Whisky! soul o' plays an' pranks!
Accept a Bardie's gratefu' thanks!
When wanting thee, what tuneless cranks
       Are my poor verses!
Thou comes—they rattle i' their ranks
       At ither's arses!

XIX

Thee, Ferintosh! O sadly lost!
Scotland lament frae coast to coast!
Now colic grips, an' barkin hoast
       May kill us a';
For loyal Forbés' chartered boast
       Is taen awa!

XX

Thae curst horse-leeches o' th' Excise,
Wha mak the whisky stells their prize!
Haud up thy han', Deil! ance, twice, thrice!
       There, seize the blinkers!
An' bake them up in brunstane pies
       For poor damn'd drinkers.

XXI

Fortune! if thou 'll but gie me still
Hale breeks, a scone, an' whisky gill,
An' rowth o' rhyme to rave at will,
                    Tak a' the rest,
An' deal 't about as thy blind skill
                    Directs thee best.

The Holy Fair

A robe of seeming truth and trust
    Hid crafty observation;
And secret hung, with poison'd crust,
    The dirk of defamation:
A mask that like the gorget show'd,
    Dye-varying on the pigeon;
And for a mantle large and broad,
    He wrapt him in Religion.
                    Hypocrisy à-la-mode.

I

Upon a simmer Sunday morn,
    When Nature's face is fair,
I walkèd forth to view the corn,
    An' snuff the caller air.
The rising sun, owre Galston Muirs,
    Wi' glorious light was glintin;
The hares were hirplin down the furs,
    The lav'rocks they were chantin
                    Fu' sweet that day.

II

As lightsomely I glowr'd abroad,
    To see a scene sae gay,
Three hizzies, early at the road,
    Cam skelpin up the way.
Twa had manteeles o' dolefu' black,
    But ane wi' lyart lining;
The third, that gaed a wee a-back,
    Was in the fashion shining
                    Fu' gay that day.

III

The twa appear'd like sisters twin,
    In feature, form, an' claes;
Their visage wither'd, lang an' thin,
    An' sour as onie slaes:
The third cam up, hap-step-an'-lowp,
    As light as onie lambie,
An' wi' a curchie low did stoop,
    As soon as e'er she saw me,
            Fu' kind that day.

IV

Wi' bonnet aff, quoth I, "Sweet lass,
    I think ye seem to ken me;
I 'm sure I 've seen that bonie face,
    But yet I canna name ye."
Quo' she, an' laughin as she spak,
    An' taks me by the han's,
"Ye, for my sake, hae gi'en the feck
    Of a' the Ten Comman's
            A screed some day.

V

"My name is Fun—your cronie dear,
    The nearest friend ye hae;
An' this is Superstition here,
    An' that 's Hypocrisy.
I 'm gaun to Mauchline Holy Fair,
    To spend an hour in daffin:
Gin ye 'll go there, yon runkl'd pair,
    We will get famous laughin
            At them this day."

VI

Quoth I, "Wi' a' my heart, I 'll do 't;
    I 'll get my Sunday's sark on,
An' meet you on the holy spot;
    Faith, we 'se hae fine remarkin!"
Then I gaed hame at crowdie-time,
    An' soon I made me ready;

For roads were clad, frae side to side,
    Wi' monie a wearie body,
                In droves that day.

VII

Here farmers gash, in ridin graith,
    Gaed hoddin by their cotters;
There swankies young, in braw braid-claith,
    Are springin owre the gutters.
The lasses, skelpin barefit, thrang,
    In silks an' scarlets glitter;
Wi' sweet-milk cheese, in monie a whang,
    An' farls, bak'd wi' butter,
                Fu' crump that day.

VIII

When by the plate we set our nose,
    Weel heapèd up wi' ha'pence,
A greedy glowr black-bonnet throws,
    An' we maun draw our tippence.
Then in we go to see the show:
    On ev'ry side they 're gath'rin;
Some carryin dails, some chairs an' stools,
    An' some are busy bleth'rin
                Right loud that day.

IX

Here stands a shed to fend the show'rs,
    An' screen our countra gentry;
There Racer Jess, an' twa-three whores,
    Are blinkin at the entry.
Here sits a raw o' tittlin jads,
    Wi' heavin breasts an' bare neck;
An' there a batch o' wabster lads,
    Blackguardin frae Kilmarnock,
                For fun this day.

X

Here some are thinkin on their sins,
    An' some upo' their claes;
Ane curses feet that fyl'd his shins,

Anither sighs an' prays:
On this hand sits a chosen swatch,
   Wi' screw'd-up, grace-proud faces;
On that a set o' chaps, at watch,
   Thrang winkin on the lasses
               To chairs that day.

XI

O happy is that man an' blest!
   Nae wonder that it pride him!
Whase ain dear lass, that he likes best,
   Comes clinkin down beside him!
Wi' arm repos'd on the chair back,
   He sweetly does compose him;
Which, by degrees, slips round her neck,
   An 's loof upon her bosom,
               Unkend that day.

XII

Now a' the congregation o'er
   Is silent expectation;
For Moodie speels the holy door,
   Wi' tidings o' damnation:
Should Hornie, as in ancient days,
   'Mang sons o' God present him;
The vera sight o' Moodie's face
   To 's ain het hame had sent him
               Wi' fright that day.

XIII

Hear how he clears the points o' Faith
   Wi' rattlin and thumpin!
Now meekly calm, now wild in wrath,
   He 's stampin, an' he 's jumpin!
His lengthen'd chin, his turn'd-up snout,
   His eldritch squeel an' gestures,
O how they fire the heart devout—
   Like cantharidian plaisters
              On sic a day.

XIV

But hark! the tent has chang'd its voice;
　　There 's peace an' rest nae langer;
For a' the real judges rise,
　　They canna sit for anger:
Smith opens out his cauld harangues,
　　On practice and on morals;
An' aff the godly pour in thrangs,
　　To gie the jars an' barrels
　　　　　　　A lift that day.

XV

What signifies his barren shine,
　　Of moral pow'rs an' reason?
His English style, an' gesture fine
　　Are a' clean out o' season.
Like Socrates or Antonine,
　　Or some auld pagan heathen,
The moral man he does define,
　　But ne'er a word o' faith in
　　　　　　　That 's right that day.

XVI

In guid time comes an antidote
　　Against sic poison'd nostrum;
For Peebles, frae the water-fit,
　　Ascends the holy rostrum:
See, up he 's got the word o' God,
　　An' meek an' mim has view'd it,
While Common-sense has taen the road,
　　An' aff, an' up the Cowgate
　　　　　　　Fast, fast that day.

XVII

Wee Miller niest, the guard relieves,
　　An' orthodoxy raibles,
Tho' in his heart he weel believes,
　　An' thinks it auld wives' fables:
But faith! the birkie wants a manse:
　　So, cannilie he hums them;

Altho' his carnal wit an' sense
   Like hafflins-wise o'ercomes him
           At times that day.

XVIII

Now butt an' ben the change-house fills,
   Wi' yill-caup commentators;
Here 's crying out for bakes an' gills,
   An' there the pint-stowp clatters;
While thick an' thrang, an' loud an' lang,
   Wi' logic an' wi' Scripture,
They raise a din, that in the end
   Is like to breed a rupture
            O' wrath that day.

XIX

Leeze me on drink! it gies us mair
   Than either school or college;
It kindles wit, it waukens lear,
   It pangs us fou o' knowledge:
Be 't whisky-gill or penny wheep,
   Or onie stronger potion,
It never fails, on drinkin deep,
   To kittle up our notion,
            By night or day.

XX

The lads an' lasses, blythely bent
   To mind baith saul an' body,
Sit round the table, weel content,
   An' steer about the toddy:
On this ane's dress, an' that ane's leuk,
   They 're makin observations;
While some are cozie i' the neuk,
   An' formin assignations
            To meet some day.

XXI

But now the Lord's ain trumpet touts,
   Till a' the hills are rairin,

And echoes back return the shouts;
 Black Russell is na spairin:
His piercin words, like Highlan' swords,
 Divide the joints an' marrow;
His talk o' Hell, whare devils dwell,
 Our verra "sauls does harrow"
     Wi' fright that day!

XXII

A vast, unbottom'd, boundless pit,
 Fill'd fou o' lowin brunstane,
Whase ragin flame, an' scorchin heat,
 Wad melt the hardest whun-stane!
The half-asleep start up wi' fear,
 An' think they hear it roarin;
When presently it does appear,
 'T was but some neebor snorin
     Asleep that day.

XXIII

'T wad be owre lang a tale to tell,
 How monie stories past;
An' how they crouded to the yill,
 When they were a' dismist;
How drink gaed round, in cogs an' caups,
 Amang the furms an' benches;
An' cheese an' bread, frae women's laps,
 Was dealt about in lunches,
     An' dawds that day.

XXIV

In comes a gawsie, gash guidwife,
 An' sits down by the fire,
Syne draws her kebbuck an' her knife;
 The lasses they are shyer:
The auld guidmen, about the grace,
 Frae side to side they bother;
Till some ane by his bonnet lays,
 An' gies them 't, like a tether,
     Fu' lang that day.

XXV

Waesucks! for him that gets nae lass,
    Or lasses that hae naething!
Sma' need has he to say a grace,
    Or melvie his braw claithing!
O wives, be mindfu', ance yoursel,
    How bonie lads ye wanted,
An' dinna for a kebbuck-heel
    Let lasses be affronted
                    On sic a day!

XXVI

Now Clinkumbell, wi' rattlin tow,
    Begins to jow an' croon;
Some swagger hame the best they dow,
    Some wait the afternoon.
At slaps the billies halt a blink,
    Till lasses strip their shoon:
Wi' faith an' hope, an' love an' drink,
    They 're a' in famous tune
                    For crack that day.

XXVII

How monie hearts this day converts
    O' sinners and o' lasses!
Their hearts o' stane, gin night, are gane
    As saft as onie flesh is:
There 's some are fou o' love divine;
    There 's some are fou o' brandy;
An' monie jobs that day begin,
    May end in houghmagandie
                    Some ither day.

Address to the Deil

O Prince! O Chief of many thronèd pow'rs!
That led th' embattl'd seraphim to war.
                    MILTON.

I

O thou! whatever title suit thee—
Auld Hornie, Satan, Nick, or Clootie—
Wha in yon cavern grim an' sootie,
                    Clos'd under hatches,
Spairges about the brunstane cootie,
                    To scaud poor wretches!

II

Hear me, Auld Hangie, for a wee,
An' let poor damnèd bodies be;
I 'm sure sma' pleasure it can gie,
                    Ev'n to a deil,
To skelp an' scaud poor dogs like me
                    An' hear us squeel.

III

Great is thy pow'r an' great thy fame;
Far kend an' noted is thy name;
An' tho' yon lowin heugh 's thy hame,
                    Thou travels far;
An' faith! thou 's neither lag, nor lame,
                    Nor blate, nor scaur.

IV

Whyles, ranging like a roarin lion,
For prey, a' holes an' corners trying;
Whyles, on the strong-wing'd tempest flyin,
                    Tirlin the kirks;
Whyles, in the human bosom pryin,
                    Unseen thou lurks.

V

I 've heard my rev'rend graunie say,
In lanely glens ye like to stray;

Or, where auld ruin'd castles grey
         Nod to the moon,
Ye fright the nightly wand'rer's way
         Wi' eldritch croon.

VI

When twilight did my graunie summon,
To say her pray'rs, douce, honest woman!
Aft yont the dyke she 's heard you bummin,
         Wi' eerie drone;
Or, rustlin, thro' the boortrees comin,
         Wi' heavy groan.

VII

Ae dreary, windy, winter night,
The star shot down wi' sklentin light,
Wi' you mysel, I gat a fright:
         Ayont the lough,
Ye, like a rash-buss, stood in sight,
         Wi' waving sugh.

VIII

The cudgel in my nieve did shake,
Each bristl'd hair stood like a stake;
When wi' an eldritch, stoor "quaick, quaick,"
         Amang the springs,
Awa ye squatter'd like a drake,
         On whistling wings.

IX

Let warlocks grim, an' wither'd hags,
Tell how wi' you, on ragweed nags,
They skim the muirs an' dizzy crags,
         Wi' wicked speed;
And in kirk-yards renew their leagues,
         Owre howkit dead.

X

Thence, countra wives, wi' toil an' pain,
May plunge an' plunge the kirn in vain;

For O! the yellow treasure 's taen
            By witching skill;
An' dawtit, twal-pint hawkie 's gaen
            As yell 's the bill.

XI

Thence, mystic knots mak great abuse
On young guidmen, fond, keen an' croose;
When the best wark-lume i' the house,
            By cantraip wit,
Is instant made no worth a louse,
            Just at the bit.

XII

When thowes dissolve the snawy hoord,
An' float the jinglin icy boord,
Then, water-kelpies haunt the foord,
            By your direction,
An' nighted trav'llers are allur'd
            To their destruction.

XIII

And aft your moss-traversing spunkies
Decoy the wight that late an' drunk is:
The bleezin, curst, mischievous monkies
            Delude his eyes,
Till in some miry slough he sunk is,
            Ne'er mair to rise.

XIV

When Masons' mystic word an' grip
In storms an' tempests raise you up,
Some cock or cat your rage maun stop,
            Or, strange to tell!
The youngest brother ye wad whip
            Aff straught to hell.

XV

Lang syne in Eden's bonie yard,
When youthfu' lovers first were pair'd,
An' all the soul of love they shar'd,
            The raptur'd hour,

Sweet on the fragrant flow'ry swaird,
                    In shady bow'r:

XVI

Then you, ye auld, snick-drawing dog!
Ye cam to Paradise incog,
An' play'd on man a cursed brogue
                    (Black be your fa'!),
An' gied the infant warld a shog,
                    'Maist ruin'd a'.

XVII

D' ye mind that day when in a bizz
Wi' reekit duds, an' reestit gizz,
Ye did present your smoutie phiz
                    'Mang better folk;
An' sklented on the man of Uzz
                    Your spitefu' joke?

XVIII

An' how ye gat him i' your thrall,
An' brak him out o' house an' hal',
While scabs an' botches did him gall,
                    Wi' bitter claw;
An' lows'd his ill-tongu'd wicked scaul—
                    Was warst ava?

XIX

But a' your doings to rehearse,
Your wily snares an' fechtin fierce,
Sin' that day Michael did you pierce
                    Down to this time,
Wad ding a Lallan tongue, or Erse,
                    In prose or rhyme.

XX

An' now, Auld Cloots, I ken ye 're thinkin,
A certain Bardie's rantin, drinkin,
Some luckless hour will send him linkin,
                    To your black Pit;
But, faith! he 'll turn a corner jinkin,
                    An' cheat you yet.

XXI

But fare-you-weel, Auld Nickie-Ben!
O, wad ye tak a thought an' men'!
Ye aiblins might—I dinna ken—
   Still hae a stake:
I 'm wae to think upo' yon den,
   Ev'n for your sake!

The Death and Dying Words of Poor Mailie,

THE AUTHOR'S ONLY PET YOWE:
AN UNCO MOURNFU' TALE

As Mailie, an' her lambs thegither,
Was ae day nibblin on the tether,
Upon her cloot she coost a hitch,
An' owre she warsl'd in the ditch:
There, groanin, dying, she did lie,
When Hughoc he cam doytin by.

Wi' glowrin een, an' lifted han's
Poor Hughoc like a statue stan's;
He saw her days were near-hand ended,
But, wae 's my heart! he could na mend it!
He gapèd wide, but naething spak.
At length poor Mailie silence brak:—

"O thou, whase lamentable face
Appears to mourn my woefu' case!
My dying words attentive hear,
An' bear them to my Master dear.

"Tell him, if e'er again he keep
As muckle gear as buy a sheep—
O, bid him never tie them mair,
Wi' wicked strings o' hemp or hair!
But ca' them out to park or hill,
An' let them wander at their will:
So may his flock increase, an' grow
To scores o' lambs, an' packs o' woo'!

"Tell him, he was a Master kin',
An' ay was guid to me an' mine;

An' now my dying charge I gie him,
My helpless lambs, I trust them wi' him.

  "O, bid him save their harmless lives,
Frae dogs, an' tods, an' butchers' knives!
But gie them guid cow-milk their fill,
Till they be fit to fend themsel;
An' tent them duly, e'en an' morn,
Wi' teats o' hay an' ripps o' corn.

  "An' may they never learn the gaets,
Of ither vile, wanrestfu' pets—
To slink thro' slaps, an' reave an' steal,
At stacks o' pease, or stocks o' kail!
So may they, like their great forbears,
For monie a year come thro' the sheers:
So wives will gie them bits o' bread,
An' bairns greet for them when they 're dead.

  "My poor toop-lamb, my son an' heir,
O, bid him breed him up wi' care!
An' if he live to be a beast,
To pit some havins in his breast!
An' warn him—what I winna name—
To stay content wi' yowes at hame;
An' no to rin an' wear his cloots,
Like other menseless, graceless brutes.

  "An' niest, my yowie, silly thing;
Gude keep thee frae a tether string!
O, may thou ne'er forgather up,
Wi' onie blastit, moorland toop;
But ay keep mind to moop an' mell,
Wi' sheep o' credit like thysel!

  "And now, my bairns, wi' my last breath,
I lea'e my blessin wi' you baith:
An' when you think upo' your mither,
Mind to be kind to ane anither.

  "Now, honest Hughoc, dinna fail,
To tell my master a' my tale;
An' bid him burn this cursed tether,
An' for thy pains thou 'se get my blether."

This said, poor Mailie turn'd her head,
An' clos'd her een amang the dead!

The Cotter's Saturday Night

INSCRIBED TO R. AIKEN, ESQ.

Let not Ambition mock their useful toil,
   Their homely joys, and destiny obscure;
Nor Grandeur hear, with a disdainful smile,
   The short and simple annals of the poor.
                         GRAY

I

My lov'd, my honor'd, much respected friend!
   No mercenary bard his homage pays;
With honest pride, I scorn each selfish end,
   My dearest meed, a friend's esteem and praise:
   To you I sing, in simple Scottish lays,
The lowly train in life's sequester'd scene;
   The native feelings strong, the guileless ways;
What Aiken in a cottage would have been;
Ah! tho' his worth unknown, far happier there I ween!

II

November chill blaws loud wi' angry sugh;
   The short'ning winter-day is near a close;
The miry beasts retreating frae the pleugh;
   The black'ning trains o' craws to their repose:
   The toil-worn Cotter frae his labor goes—
This night his weekly moil is at an end,
   Collects his spades, his mattocks, and his hoes,
Hoping the morn in ease and rest to spend,
And weary, o'er the moor, his course does hameward bend.

III

At length his lonely cot appears in view,
   Beneath the shelter of an aged tree;
Th' expectant wee-things, toddlin, stacher through

To meet their dad, wi' flichterin' noise and glee.
    His wee bit ingle, blinkin bonilie,
His clean hearth-stane, his thrifty wifie's smile,
    The lisping infant, prattling on his knee,
Does a' his weary kiaugh and care beguile,
And makes him quite forget his labor and his toil.

IV

Belyve, the elder bairns come drapping in,
    At service out, amang the farmers roun';
Some ca' the pleugh, some herd, some tentie rin
    A cannie errand to a neebor town:
    Their eldest hope, their Jenny, woman grown,
In youthfu' bloom, love sparkling in her e'e,
    Comes hame; perhaps, to shew a braw new gown,
Or deposite her sair-won penny-fee,
To help her parents dear, if they in hardship be.

V

With joy unfeign'd, brothers and sisters meet,
    And each for other's weelfare kindly spiers:
The social hours, swift-wing'd, unnotic'd fleet;
    Each tells the uncos that he sees or hears.
    The parents partial eye their hopeful years;
Anticipation forward points the view;
    The mother, wi' her needle and her sheers,
Gars auld claes look amaist as weel 's the new;
The father mixes a' wi' admonition due.

VI

Their master's and their mistress's command
    The younkers a' are warnèd to obey;
And mind their labours wi' an eydent hand,
    And ne'er, tho' out o' sight, to jauk or play:
    "And O! be sure to fear the Lord alway,
And mind your duty, duly, morn and night;
    Lest in temptation's path ye gang astray,
Implore His counsel and assisting might:
They never sought in vain that sought the Lord aright."

VII

But hark! a rap comes gently to the door;
   Jenny, wha kens the meaning o' the same,
Tells how a neebor lad came o'er the moor,
   To do some errands, and convoy her hame.
   The wily mother sees the conscious flame
Sparkle in Jenny's e'e, and flush her cheek;
   With heart-struck anxious care, enquires his name,
While Jenny hafflins is afraid to speak;
Weel-pleas'd the mother hears, it 's nae wild, worthless rake.

VIII

With kindly welcome, Jenny brings him ben;
   A strappin' youth, he takes the mother's eye;
Blythe Jenny sees the visit 's no ill taen;
   The father cracks of horses, pleughs, and kye.
   The youngster's artless heart o'erflows wi' joy,
But blate and laithfu', scarce can weel behave;
   The mother, wi' a woman's wiles, can spy
What makes the youth sae bashfu' and sae grave;
Weel-pleas'd to think her bairn 's respected like the lave.

IX

O happy love! where love like this is found:
   O heart-felt raptures! bliss beyond compare!
I 've pacèd much this weary, mortal round,
   And sage experience bids me this declare:—
   "If Heaven a draught of heavenly pleasure spare,
One cordial in this melancholy vale,
   'T is when a youthful, loving, modest pair,
In other's arms, breathe out the tender tale
Beneath the milk-white thorn that scents the ev'ning gale."

X

Is there, in human form, that bears a heart,
   A wretch! a villain! lost to love and truth!
That can, with studied, sly, ensnaring art,
   Betray sweet Jenny's unsuspecting youth?
   Curse on his perjur'd arts! dissembling, smooth!
Are honor, virtue, conscience, all exil'd?

Is there no pity, no relenting ruth,
Points to the parents fondling o'er their child?
Then paints the ruin'd maid, and their distraction wild?

XI

But now the supper crowns their simple board,
　　The healsome parritch, chief o' Scotia's food;
The soupe their only hawkie does afford,
　　That 'yont the hallan snugly chows her cood;
　　The dame brings forth, in complimental mood,
To grace the lad, her weel-hain'd kebbuck, fell;
　　And aft he 's prest, and aft he ca's it guid;
The frugal wifie, garrulous, will tell,
How 't was a towmond auld, sin' lint was i' the bell.

XII

The chearfu' supper done, wi' serious face,
　　They, round the ingle, form a circle wide;
The sire turns o'er, wi' patriarchal grace,
　　The big ha'-Bible, ance his father's pride.
　　His bonnet rev'rently is laid aside,
His lyart haffets wearing thin and bare;
　　Those strains that once did sweet in Zion glide,
He wales a portion with judicious care,
And "Let us worship God!" he says, with solemn air.

XIII

They chant their artless notes in simple guise,
　　They tune their hearts, by far the noblest aim;
Perhaps *Dundee's* wild-warbling measures rise,
　　Or plaintive *Martyrs*, worthy of the name;
　　Or noble *Elgin* beets the heaven-ward flame,
The sweetest far of Scotia's holy lays:
　　Compar'd with these, Italian trills are tame;
The tickl'd ears no heart-felt raptures raise;
Nae unison hae they, with our Creator's praise.

XIV

The priest-like father reads the sacred page,
　　How Abram was the friend of God on high;

Or, Moses bade eternal warfare wage
   With Amalek's ungracious progeny;
   Or, how the royal Bard did groaning lie
Beneath the stroke of Heaven's avenging ire;
   Or Job's pathetic plaint, and wailing cry;
   Or rapt Isaiah's wild, seraphic fire;
Or other holy Seers that tune the sacred lyre.

XV

Perhaps the Christian volume is the theme:
   How guiltless blood for guilty man was shed;
How He, who bore in Heaven the second name,
   Had not on earth whereon to lay His head;
   How His first followers and servants sped;
The precepts sage they wrote to many a land:
   How he, who lone in Patmos banishèd,
Saw in the sun a mighty angel stand,
And heard great Bab'lon's doom pronounc'd by
      Heaven's command.

XVI

Then kneeling down to Heaven's Eternal King,
   The saint, the father, and the husband prays:
Hope "springs exulting on triumphant wing,"
   That thus they all shall meet in future days,
   There, ever bask in uncreated rays,
No more to sigh or shed the bitter tear,
   Together hymning their Creator's praise,
In such society, yet still more dear;
While circling Time moves round in an eternal sphere.

XVII

Compar'd with this, how poor Religion's pride,
   In all the pomp of method, and of art;
When men display to congregations wide
   Devotion's ev'ry grace, except the heart,
   The Power, incens'd, the pageant will desert,
The pompous strain, the sacerdotal stole;
   But haply, in some cottage far apart,
May hear, well-pleas'd, the language of the soul,
And in His Book of Life the inmates poor enroll.

XVIII

Then homeward all take off their sev'ral way;
     The youngling cottagers retire to rest:
The parent-pair their secret homage pay,
     And proffer up to Heaven the warm request,
     That He who stills the raven's clam'rous nest,
And decks the lily fair in flow'ry pride,
     Would, in the way His wisdom sees the best,
For them and for their little ones provide;
But, chiefly, in their hearts with Grace Divine preside.

XIX

From scenes like these, old Scotia's grandeur springs,
     That makes her lov'd at home, rever'd abroad:
Princes and lords are but the breath of kings,
     "An honest man 's the noblest work of God;"
     And certes, in fair Virtue's heavenly road,
The cottage leaves the palace far behind;
     What is a lordling's pomp? a cumbrous load,
Disguising oft the wretch of human kind,
Studied in arts of Hell, in wickedness refin'd!

XX

O Scotia! my dear, my native soil!
     For whom my warmest wish to Heaven is sent!
Long may thy hardy sons of rustic toil
     Be blest with health, and peace, and sweet content!
     And O! may Heaven their simple lives prevent
From Luxury's contagion, weak and vile!
     Then, howe'er crowns and coronets be rent,
A virtuous populace may rise the while,
And stand a wall of fire around their much-lov'd Isle.

XXI

O Thou! who pour'd the patriotic tide,
     That stream'd thro' Wallace's undaunted heart,
Who dar'd to, nobly, stem tyrannic pride,
     Or nobly die, the second glorious part:
     (The patriot's God, peculiarly Thou art,
His friend, inspirer, guardian, and reward!)

O never, never Scotia's realm desert;
But still the patriot, and the patriot-bard
In bright succession raise, her ornament and guard!

To a Mouse

ON TURNING HER UP IN HER NEST WITH
THE PLOUGH, NOVEMBER, 1785

I

Wee, sleekit, cowrin, tim'rous beastie,
O, what a panic 's in thy breastie!
Thou need na start awa sae hasty
   Wi' bickering brattle!
I wad be laith to rin an' chase thee,
   Wi' murdering pattle!

II

I 'm truly sorry man's dominion
Has broken Nature's social union,
An' justifies that ill opinion
   Which makes thee startle
At me, thy poor, earth-born companion
   An' fellow mortal!

III

I doubt na, whyles, but thou may thieve;
What then? poor beastie, thou maun live.
A daimen icker in a thrave
   'S a sma' request;
I 'll get a blessin wi' the lave,
   An' never miss 't!

IV

Thy wee-bit housie, too, in ruin!
Its silly wa's the win's are strewin!
An' naething, now, to big a new ane,
   O' foggage green!
An' bleak December's win's ensuin,
   Baith snell an' keen!

V

Thou saw the fields laid bare an' waste,
An' weary winter comin fast,
An' cozie here, beneath the blast,
        Thou thought to dwell,
Till crash! the cruel coulter past
         Out thro' thy cell.

VI

That wee bit heap o' leaves an' stibble,
Has cost thee monie a weary nibble!
Now thou 's turned out, for a' thy trouble,
        But house or hald,
To thole the winter's sleety dribble,
         An' cranreuch cauld!

VII

But Mousie, thou art no thy lane,
In proving foresight may be vain:
The best-laid schemes o' mice an' men
        Gang aft agley,
An' lea'e us nought but grief an' pain,
         For promis'd joy!

VIII

Still thou art blest, compared wi' me!
The present only toucheth thee:
But och! I backward cast my e'e,
        On prospects drear!
An' forward, tho' I canna see,
         I guess an' fear!

To a Mountain Daisy

ON TURNING ONE DOWN WITH THE
PLOUGH IN APRIL, 1786

I

Wee, modest, crimson-tippèd flow'r,
Thou 's met me in an evil hour;

For I maun crush amang the stoure
        Thy slender stem:
To spare thee now is past my pow'r,
        Thou bonie gem.

II

Alas! it 's no thy neebor sweet,
The bonie lark, companion meet,
Bending thee 'mang the dewy weet,
        Wi' spreckl'd breast!
When upward-springing, blythe, to greet
        The purpling east.

III

Cauld blew the bitter-biting north
Upon thy early, humble birth;
Yet cheerfully thou glinted forth
        Amid the storm,
Scarce rear'd above the parent-earth
        Thy tender form.

IV

The flaunting flow'rs our gardens yield,
High shelt'ring woods and wa's maun shield;
But thou, beneath the random bield
        O' clod or stane,
Adorns the histie stibble-field,
        Unseen, alane.

V

There, in thy scanty mantle clad,
Thy snawie bosom sun-ward spread,
Thou lifts thy unassuming head
        In humble guise;
But now the share uptears thy bed,
        And low thou lies!

VI

Such is the fate of artless maid,
Sweet flow'ret of the rural shade!

By love's simplicity betray'd,
   And guileless trust;
Till she, like thee, all soil'd, is laid
   Low i' the dust.

VII

Such is the fate of simple Bard,
On Life's rough ocean luckless starr'd!
Unskilful he to note the card
   Of prudent lore,
Till billows rage, and gales blow hard,
   And whelm him o'er!

VIII

Such fate to suffering Worth is giv'n,
Who long with wants and woes has striv'n,
By human pride or cunning driv'n
   To mis'ry's brink;
Till, wrench'd of ev'ry stay but Heav'n,
   He, ruin'd, sink!

IX

Ev'n thou who mourn'st the Daisy's fate,
That fate is thine—no distant date;
Stern Ruin's plough-share drives elate,
   Full on thy bloom,
Till crush'd beneath the furrow's weight
   Shall be thy doom!

Epistle to a Young Friend

May——1786.

I

I lang hae thought, my youthfu' friend,
 A something to have sent you,
Tho' it should serve nae ither end
 Than just a kind memento:
But how the subject-theme may gang,

Let time and chance determine:
Perhaps it may turn out a sang;
    Perhaps, turn out a sermon.

II

Ye 'll try the world soon, my lad;
    And, Andrew dear, believe me,
Ye 'll find mankind an unco squad,
    And muckle they may grieve ye:
For care and trouble set your thought,
    Ev'n when your end 's attainèd:
And a' your views may come to nought,
    Where ev'ry nerve is strainèd.

III

I 'll no say, men are villains a':
    The real, harden'd wicked,
Wha hae nae check but human law,
    Are to a few restricked;
But, och! mankind are unco weak
    An' little to be trusted;
If Self the wavering balance shake,
    It 's rarely right adjusted!

IV

Yet they wha fa' in Fortune's strife,
    Their fate we should na censure;
For still, th' important end of life
    They equally may answer:
A man may hae an honest heart,
    Tho' poortith hourly stare him;
A man may tak a neebor's part,
    Yet hae nae cash to spare him.

V

Ay free, aff han', your story tell,
    When wi' a bosom cronie;
But still keep something to yoursel
    Ye scarcely tell to onie:
Conceal yoursel as weel 's ye can

Frae critical dissection:
But keek thro' ev'ry other man
    Wi' sharpen'd, sly inspection.

VI

The sacred lowe o' weel-plac'd love,
    Luxuriantly indulge it;
But never tempt th' illicit rove,
    Tho' naething should divulge it:
I waive the quantum o' the sin,
    The hazard of concealing;
But, och! it hardens a' within,
    And petrifies the feeling!

VII

To catch Dame Fortune's golden smile,
    Assiduous wait upon her;
And gather gear by ev'ry wile
    That 's justify'd by honour:
Not for to hide it in a hedge,
    Nor for a train-attendant;
But for the glorious privilege
    Of being independent.

VIII

The fear o' Hell 's a hangman's whip
    To haud the wretch in order;
But where ye feel your honour grip,
    Let that ay be your border:
Its slightest touches, instant pause—
    Debar a' side-pretences;
And resolutely keep its laws,
    Uncaring consequences.

IX

The great Creator to revere
    Must sure become the creature;
But still the preaching cant forbear,
    And ev'n the rigid feature:
Yet ne'er with wits profane to range

Be complaisance extended;
An atheist-laugh 's a poor exchange
    For Deity offended!

X

When ranting round in Pleasure's ring,
    Religion may be blinded;
Or if she gie a random sting,
    It may be little minded;
But when on Life we 're tempest-driv'n—
    A conscience but a canker—
A correspondence fix'd wi' Heav'n
    Is sure a noble anchor!

XI

Adieu, dear, amiable youth!
    Your heart can ne'er be wanting!
May prudence, fortitude, and truth,
    Erect your brow undaunting!
In ploughman phrase, "God send you speed,"
    Still daily to grow wiser;
And may ye better reck the rede,
    Than ever did th' adviser!

To a Louse

ON SEEING ONE ON A LADY'S
BONNET AT CHURCH

I

Ha! whare ye gaun, ye crowlin ferlie?
Your impudence protects you sairly,
I canna say but ye strunt rarely
                Owre gauze and lace,
Tho' faith! I fear ye dine but sparely
                On sic a place.

II

Ye ugly, creepin, blastit wonner,
Detested, shunn'd by saunt an' sinner,

How daur ye set your fit upon her—
        Sae fine a lady!
Gae somewhere else and seek your dinner
        On some poor body.

III

Swith! in some beggar's hauffet squattle:
There ye may creep, and sprawl, and sprattle,
Wi' ither kindred, jumping cattle,
        In shoals and nations;
Whare horn nor bane ne'er daur unsettle
        Your thick plantations.

IV

Now haud you there! ye 're out o' sight,
Below the fatt'rils, snug an' tight;
Na, faith ye yet! ye 'll no be right,
        Till ye 've got on it—
The vera tapmost, tow'ring height
        O' Miss's bonnet.

V

My sooth! right bauld ye set your nose out,
As plump an' grey as onie grozet:
O for some rank, mercurial rozet,
        Or fell, red smeddum,
I 'd gie ye sic a hearty dose o 't,
        Wad dress your droddum.

VI

I wad na been surpris'd to spy
You on an auld wife's flainen toy;
Or aiblins some bit duddie boy,
        On 's wyliecoat;
But Miss's fine Lunardi! fye!
        How daur ye do 't?

VII

O Jenny, dinna toss your head,
An' set your beauties a' abread!

Ye little ken what cursèd speed
             The blastie 's makin!
Thae winks an' finger-ends, I dread,
             Are notice takin!

VIII

O wad some Power the giftie gie us
To see oursels as ithers see us!
It wad frae monie a blunder free us,
             An' foolish notion:
What airs in dress an' gait wad lea'e us,
             An' ev'n devotion!

Song

TUNE: *Corn Rigs*

I

It was upon a Lammas night,
  When corn rigs are bonie,
Beneath the moon's unclouded light,
  I held awa to Annie;
The time flew by, wi' tentless heed;
  Till, 'tween the late and early,
Wi' sma' persuasion she agreed
  To see me thro' the barley.
        Corn rigs, an' barley rigs,
          An' corn rigs are bonie:
          I 'll ne'er forget that happy night,
            Amang the rigs wi' Annie.

II

The sky was blue, the wind was still,
  The moon was shining clearly;
I set her down, wi' right good will,
  Amang the rigs o' barley:
I ken't her heart was a' my ain;
  I lov'd her most sincerely;

I kiss'd her owre and owre again,
    Amang the rigs o' barley.

III

I lock'd her in my fond embrace;
    Her heart was beating rarely:
My blessings on that happy place,
    Amang the rigs o' barley!
But by the moon and stars so bright,
    That shone that hour so clearly!
She ay shall bless that happy night
    Amang the rigs o' barley.

IV

I hae been blythe wi' comrades dear;
    I hae been merry drinking;
I hae been joyfu' gath'rin gear;
    I hae been happy thinking:
But a' the pleasures e'er I saw,
    Tho' three times doubl'd fairly—
That happy night was worth them a',
    Amang the rigs o' barley.
        Corn rigs, an' barley rigs,
           An' corn rigs are bonie:
        I 'll ne'er forget that happy night,
           Amang the rigs wi' Annie.

Address to the Unco Guid

OR THE RIGIDLY RIGHTEOUS

    My Son, these maxims make a rule,
        An' lump them ay thegither:
    The Rigid Righteous is a fool,
        The Rigid Wise anither;
    The cleanest corn that e'er was dight
        May hae some pyles o' caff in;
    So ne'er a fellow-creature slight
        For random fits o' daffin.
                SOLOMON (Eccles. vii. 16)

I

O ye, wha are sae guid yoursel,
    Sae pious and sae holy,
Ye 've nought to do but mark and tell
    Your neebours' fauts and folly;
Whase life is like a weel-gaun mill,
    Supplied wi' store o' water;
The heapet happer 's ebbing still,
    An' still the clap plays clatter!

II

Hear me, ye venerable core,
    As counsel for poor mortals
That frequent pass douce Wisdom's door
    For glaikit Folly's portals:
I for their thoughtless, careless sakes
    Would here propone defences—
Their donsie tricks, their black mistakes,
    Their failings and mischances.

III

Ye see your state wi' theirs compared,
    And shudder at the niffer;
But cast a moment's fair regard,
    What makes the mighty differ?
Discount what scant occasion gave;
    That purity ye pride in;
And (what 's aft mair than a' the lave)
    Your better art o' hidin.

IV

Think, when your castigated pulse
    Gies now and then a wallop,
What ragings must his veins convulse,
    That still eternal gallop!
Wi' wind and tide fair i' your tail,
    Right on ye scud your sea-way;
But in the teeth o' baith to sail,
    It makes an unco lee-way.

V

See Social-life and Glee sit down
    All joyous and unthinking,
Till, quite transmugrify'd, they 're grown
    Debauchery and Drinking:
O, would they stay to calculate,
    Th' eternal consequences,
Or—your more dreaded hell to state—
    Damnation of expenses!

VI

Ye high, exalted, virtuous dames,
    Tied up in godly laces,
Before ye gie poor Frailty names,
    Suppose a change o' cases:
A dear-lov'd lad, convenience snug,
    A treach'rous inclination—
But, let me whisper i' your lug,
    Ye 're aiblins nae temptation.

VII

Then gently scan your brother man,
    Still gentler sister woman;
Tho' they may gang a kennin wrang,
    To step aside is human:
One point must still be greatly dark,
    The moving *why* they do it;
And just as lamely can ye mark
    How far perhaps they rue it.

VIII

Who made the heart, 't is He alone
    Decidedly can try us:
He knows each chord, its various tone,
    Each spring, its various bias:
Then at the balance let 's be mute,
    We never can adjust it;
What 's done we partly may compute,
    But know not what 's resisted.

Green Grow the Rashes, O

CHORUS

> Green grow the rashes, O;
> Green grow the rashes, O;
> The sweetest hours that e'er I spend,
> Are spent among the lasses, O.

I

> There 's nought but care on ev'ry han',
> In every hour that passes, O:
> What signifies the life o' man,
> An' 't were nae for the lasses, O.

II

> The war'ly race may riches chase,
> An' riches still may fly them, O;
> An' tho' at last they catch them fast,
> Their hearts can ne'er enjoy them, O.

III

> But gie me a cannie hour at e'en,
> My arms about my dearie, O,
> An' war'ly cares an' war'ly men
> May a' gae tapsalteerie, O!

IV

> For you sae douce, ye sneer at this;
> Ye 're nought but senseless asses, O;
> The wisest man the warl' e'er saw,
> He dearly lov'd the lasses, O.

V

> Auld Nature swears, the lovely dears
> Her noblest work she classes, O:
> Her prentice han' she try'd on man,
> An' then she made the lasses, O.

CHORUS

> Green grow the rashes, O;
> Green grow the rashes, O;
> The sweetest hours that e'er I spend,
> Are spent among the lasses, O.

Tam o' Shanter

A TALE

Of Brownyis and of Bogillis full is this Buke.
                              GAWIN DOUGLAS.

When chapman billies leave the street,
And drouthy neebors neebors meet;
As market-days are wearing late,
An' folk begin to tak the gate;
While we sit bousing at the nappy,
An' getting fou and unco happy,
We think na on the lang Scots miles,
The mosses, waters, slaps, and styles,
That lie between us and our hame,
Whare sits our sulky, sullen dame,
Gathering her brows like gathering storm,
Nursing her wrath to keep it warm.

   This truth fand honest Tam o' Shanter,
As he frae Ayr ae night did canter:
(Auld Ayr, wham ne'er a town surpasses,
For honest men and bonie lasses).

   O Tam, had'st thou but been sae wise,
As taen thy ain wife Kate's advice!
She tauld thee weel thou was a skellum,
A blethering, blustering, drunken blellum;
That frae November till October,
Ae market-day thou was nae sober;
That ilka melder wi' the miller,
Thou sat as lang as thou had siller;
That ev'ry naig was ca'd a shoe on,
The smith and thee gat roaring fou on;
That at the Lord's house, even on Sunday,

Thou drank wi' Kirkton Jean till Monday.
She prophesied, that, late or soon,
Thou would be found deep drown'd in Doon,
Or catch'd wi' warlocks in the mirk
By Alloway's auld, haunted kirk.

Ah! gentle dames, it gars me greet,
To think how monie counsels sweet,
How monie lengthen'd, sage advices
The husband frae the wife despises!

But to our tale : Ae market-night,
Tam had got planted unco right,
Fast by an ingle, bleezing finely,
Wi' reaming swats, that drank divinely;
And at his elbow, Souter Johnie,
His ancient, trusty, drouthy cronie:
Tam lo'ed him like a very brither;
They had been fou for weeks thegither.
The night drave on wi' sangs and clatter;
And ay the ale was growing better:
The landlady and Tam grew gracious
Wi' secret favours, sweet and precious:
The Souter tauld his queerest stories;
The landlord's laugh was ready chorus:
The storm without might rair and rustle,
Tam did na mind the storm a whistle.

Care, mad to see a man sae happy,
E'en drown'd himsel amang the nappy.
As bees flee hame wi' lades o' treasure,
The minutes wing'd their way wi' pleasure:
Kings may be blest but Tam was glorious,
O'er a' the ills o' life victorious!

But pleasures are like poppies spread:
You seize the flow'r, its bloom is shed;
Or like the snow falls in the river,
A moment white—then melts for ever;
Or like the borealis race,
That flit ere you can point their place;
Or like the rainbow's lovely form
Evanishing amid the storm.
Nae man can tether time or tide;

The hour approaches Tam maun ride:
That hour, o' night's black arch the key-stane,
That dreary hour Tam mounts his beast in;
And sic a night he taks the road in,
As ne'er poor sinner was abroad in.

The wind blew as 't wad blawn its last;
The rattling showers rose on the blast;
The speedy gleams the darkness swallow'd;
Loud, deep, and lang the thunder bellow'd:
That night, a child might understand,
The Deil had business on his hand.

Weel mounted on his gray mare Meg,
A better never lifted leg,
Tam skelpit on thro' dub and mire,
Despising wind, and rain, and fire;
Whiles holding fast his guid blue bonnet,
Whiles crooning o'er some auld Scots sonnet,
Whiles glow'ring round wi' prudent cares,
Lest bogles catch him unawares:
Kirk-Alloway was drawing nigh,
Whare ghaists and houlets nightly cry.

By this time he was cross the ford,
Whare in the snaw the chapman smoor'd;
And past the birks and meikle stane,
Whare drunken Charlie brak 's neck-bane;
And thro' the whins, and by the cairn,
Whare hunters fand the murder'd bairn;
And near the thorn, aboon the well,
Whare Mungo's mither hang'd hersel.
Before him Doon pours all his floods;
The doubling storm roars thro' the woods;
The lightnings flash from pole to pole;
Near and more near the thunders roll:
When, glimmering thro' the groaning trees,
Kirk-Alloway seem'd in a bleeze,
Thro' ilka bore the beams were glancing,
And loud resounded mirth and dancing.

Inspiring bold John Barleycorn,
What dangers thou canst make us scorn!
Wi' tippenny, we fear nae evil;

Wi' usquabae, we 'll face the Devil!
The swats sae ream'd in Tammie's noddle,
Fair play, he car'd na deils a boddle.
But Maggie stood, right sair astonish'd,
Till, by the heel and hand admonish'd,
She ventur'd forward on the light;
And, vow! Tam saw an unco sight!

Warlocks and witches in a dance:
Nae cotillion, brent new frae France,
But hornpipes, jigs, strathspeys, and reels,
Put life and mettle in their heels.
A winnock-bunker in the east,
There sat Auld Nick, in shape o' beast;
A tousie tyke, black, grim, and large,
To gie them music was his charge:
He screw'd the pipes and gart them skirl,
Till roof and rafters a' did dirl.
Coffins stood round, like open presses,
That shaw'd the dead in their last dresses;
And, by some devilish cantraip sleight,
Each in its cauld hand held a light:
By which heroic Tam was able
To note upon the haly table,
A murderer's banes, in gibbet-airns;
Twa span-lang, wee, unchristen'd bairns;
A thief new-cutted frae a rape—
Wi' his last gasp his gab did gape;
Five tomahawks wi' bluid red-rusted;
Five scymitars wi' murder crusted;
A garter which a babe had strangled;
A knife a father's throat had mangled—
Whom his ain son o' life bereft—
The grey-hairs yet stack to the heft;
Wi' mair of horrible and awefu',
Which even to name wad be unlawfu'.

As Tammie glowr'd, amaz'd, and curious,
The mirth and fun grew fast and furious;
The piper loud and louder blew,
The dancers quick and quicker flew,

They reel'd, they set, they cross'd, they cleekit,
Till ilka carlin swat and reekit,
And coost her duddies to the wark,
And linket at it in her sark!

Now Tam, O Tam! had thae been queans,
A' plump and strapping in their teens!
Their sarks, instead o' creeshie flannen,
Been snaw-white seventeen hunder linen!—
Thir breeks o' mine, my only pair,
That ance were plush, o' guid blue hair,
I wad hae gi'en them off my hurdies
For ae blink o' the bonie burdies!

But wither'd beldams, auld and droll,
Rigwoodie hags wad spean a foal,
Louping and flinging on a crummock,
I wonder did na turn thy stomach!

But Tam kend what was what fu' brawlie:
There was ae winsome wench and wawlie,
That night enlisted in the core,
Lang after kend on Carrick shore
(For monie a beast to dead she shot,
An' perish'd monie a bonie boat,
And shook baith meikle corn and bear,
And kept the country-side in fear).
Her cutty sark, o' Paisley harn,
That while a lassie she had worn,
In longitude tho' sorely scanty,
It was her best, and she was vauntie. . . .
Ah! little kend thy reverend grannie,
That sark she coft for her wee Nannie,
Wi' twa pund Scots ('t was a' her riches),
Wad ever grac'd a dance of witches!

But here my Muse her wing maun cour,
Sic flights are far beyond her power:
To sing how Nannie lap and flang
(A souple jad she was and strang),
And how Tam stood like ane bewitch'd,
And thought his very een enrich'd;

Even Satan glowr'd, and fidg'd fu' fain,
And hotch'd and blew wi' might and main;
Till first ae caper, syne anither,
Tam tint his reason a' thegither,
And roars out: "Weel done, Cutty-sark!"
And in an instant all was dark;
And scarcely had he Maggie rallied,
When out the hellish legion sallied.

As bees bizz out wi' angry fyke,
When plundering herds assail their byke;
As open pussie's mortal foes,
When, pop! she starts before their nose;
As eager runs the market-crowd,
When "Catch the thief!" resounds aloud:
So Maggie runs, the witches follow,
Wi' monie an eldritch skriech and hollo.

Ah, Tam! ah, Tam! thou 'll get thy fairin!
In hell they 'll roast thee like a herrin!
In vain thy Kate awaits thy comin!
Kate soon will be a woefu' woman!
Now, do thy speedy utmost, Meg,
And win the key-stane of the brig;
There, at them thou thy tail may toss,
A running stream they dare na cross!
But ere the key-stane she could make,
The fient a tail she had to shake;
For Nannie, far before the rest,
Hard upon noble Maggie prest,
And flew at Tam wi' furious ettle;
But little wist she Maggie's mettle!
Ae spring brought off her master hale,
But left behind her ain grey tail:
The carlin claught her by the rump,
And left poor Maggie scarce a stump.

Now, wha this tale o' truth shall read,
Ilk man, and mother's son, take heed:
Whene'er to drink you are inclin'd,
Or cutty sarks run in your mind,
Think! ye may buy the joys o'er dear:
Remember Tam o' Shanter's mare.

On the Late Captain Grose's Peregrinations thro' Scotland

COLLECTING THE ANTIQUITIES OF THAT KINGDOM

I

Hear, Land o' Cakes, and brither Scots
Frae Maidenkirk to Johnie Groat's,
If there 's a hole in a' your coats,
         I rede you tent it:
A chield 's amang you takin notes,
          And faith he 'll prent it:

II

If in your bounds ye chance to light
Upon a fine, fat, fodgel wight,
O' stature short but genius bright,
         That 's he, mark weel:
And wow! he has an unco sleight
         O' cauk and keel.

III

By some auld, houlet-haunted biggin,
Or kirk deserted by its riggin,
It 's ten to ane ye 'll find him snug in
         Some eldritch part,
Wi' deils, they say, Lord safe 's! colleaguin
         At some black art.

IV

Ilk ghaist that haunts auld ha' or chamer,
Ye gipsy-gang that deal in glamour,
And you, deep-read in hell's black grammar,
         Warlocks and witches:
Ye 'll quake at his conjúring hammer,
         Ye midnight bitches!

V

It 's tauld he was a sodger bred,
And ane wad rather fa'n than fled;

But now he 's quat the spurtle-blade
        And dog-skin wallet,
And taen the—Antiquarian trade,
        I think they call it.

VI

He has a fouth o' auld nick-nackets:
Rusty airn caps and jinglin jackets
Wad haud the Lothians three in tackets
        A towmont guid;
And parritch-pats and auld saut-backets
        Before the Flood.

VII

Of Eve's first fire he has a cinder;
Auld Tubalcain's fire-shool and fender;
That which distinguishèd the gender
        O' Balaam's ass:
A broomstick o' the witch of Endor,
        Weel shod wi' brass.

VIII

Forbye, he 'll shape you aff fu' gleg
The cut of Adam's philibeg;
The knife that nicket Abel's craig
        He 'll prove you fully,
It was a faulding jocteleg,
        Or lang-kail gullie.

IX

But wad ye see him in his glee—
For meikle glee and fun has he—
Then set him down, and twa or three
        Guid fellows wi' him;
And port, O port! shine thou a wee,
        And then ye 'll see him!

X

Now, by the Pow'rs o' verse and prose!
Thou art a dainty chield, O Grose!—

Whae'er o' thee shall ill suppose,
        They sair misca' thee;
I 'd take the rascal by the nose,
        Wad say, "Shame fa' thee."

Holy Willie's Prayer

And send the godly in a pet to pray.
        POPE.

I

O Thou that in the Heavens does dwell,
Wha, as it pleases best Thysel,
Sends ane to Heaven an' ten to Hell
        A' for Thy glory,
And no for onie guid or ill
        They 've done before Thee!

II

I bless and praise Thy matchless might,
When thousands Thou hast left in night,
That I am here before Thy sight,
        For gifts an' grace
A burning and a shining light
        To a' this place.

III

What was I, or my generation,
That I should get sic exaltation?
I, wha deserv'd most just damnation
        For broken laws
Sax thousand years ere my creation,
        Thro' Adam's cause!

IV

When from my mither's womb I fell,
Thou might hae plung'd me deep in hell
To gnash my gooms, and weep, and wail
        In burning lakes,

Whare damnèd devils roar and yell,
      Chain'd to their stakes.

V

Yet I am here, a chosen sample,
To show Thy grace is great and ample:
I 'm here a pillar o' Thy temple,
      Strong as a rock,
A guide, a buckler, and example
      To a' thy flock!

VI

But yet, O Lord! confess I must:
At times I 'm fash'd wi' fleshly lust;
An' sometimes, too, in warldly trust,
      Vile self gets in;
But Thou remembers we are dust,
      Defiled wi' sin.

VII

O Lord! yestreen, Thou kens, wi' Meg—
Thy pardon I sincerely beg—
O, may 't ne'er be a living plague
      To my dishonour!
An' I 'll ne'er lift a lawless leg
      Again upon her.

VIII

Besides, I farther maun avow—
Wi' Leezie's lass, three times, I trow—
But, Lord, that Friday I was fou,
      When I cam near her,
Or else, Thou kens, Thy servant true
      Wad never steer her.

IX

Maybe Thou lets this fleshly thorn
Buffet Thy servant e'en and morn,
Lest he owre proud and high should turn
      That he 's sae gifted:

If sae, Thy han' maun e'en be borne
   Until Thou lift it.

X

Lord, bless Thy chosen in this place,
For here Thou has a chosen race!
But God confound their stubborn face
   An' blast their name,
Wha bring Thy elders to disgrace
   An' open shame!

XI

Lord, mind Gau'n Hamilton's deserts:
He drinks, an' swears, an' plays at cartes,
Yet has sae monie takin arts
   Wi' great and sma',
Frae God's ain Priest the people's hearts
   He steals awa.

XII

And when we chasten'd him therefore,
Thou kens how he bred sic a splore,
And set the warld in a roar
   O' laughin at us:
Curse Thou his basket and his store,
   Kail an' potatoes!

XIII

Lord, hear my earnest cry and pray'r
Against that Presbyt'ry of Ayr!
Thy strong right hand, Lord, mak it bare
   Upo' their heads!
Lord, visit them, an' dinna spare,
   For their misdeeds!

XIV

O Lord, my God! that glib-tongu'd Aiken,
My vera heart and flesh are quakin
To think how we stood sweatin, shakin,
   An' pish'd wi' dread,

While he, wi' hingin lip an' snakin,
      Held up his head.

XV

Lord, in Thy day o' vengeance try him!
Lord, visit him wha did employ him!
And pass not in Thy mercy by them,
      Nor hear their pray'r,
But for Thy people's sake destroy them,
      An' dinna spare!

XVI

But, Lord, remember me and mine
Wi' mercies temporal and divine,
That I for grace an' gear may shine
      Excell'd by nane;
And a' the glory shall be Thine—
      Amen, Amen!

O, Whistle an' I 'll Come to Ye, My Lad

CHORUS

O, whistle an' I 'll come to ye, my lad!
O, whistle an' I 'll come to ye, my lad!
Tho' father an' mother an' a' should gae mad,
O, whistle an' I 'll come to ye, my lad!

I

But warily tent when ye come to court me,
And come nae unless the back-yett be a-jee;
Syne up the back-style, and let naebody see,
And come as ye were na comin to me,
And come as ye were na comin to me!

II

At kirk, or at market, whene'er ye meet me,
Gang by me as tho' that ye car'd na a flie;
But steal me a blink o' your bonie black e'e,

Yet look as ye were na lookin to me,
Yet look as ye were na lookin to me!

III

Ay vow and protest that ye care na for me,
And whyles ye may lightly my beauty a wee;
But court na anither tho' jokin ye be,
For fear that she wyle your fancy frae me,
For fear that she wyle your fancy frae me!

CHORUS

O, whistle an' I 'll come to ye, my lad!
O, whistle an' I 'll come to ye, my lad!
Tho' father an' mother an' a' should gae mad,
O, whistle an' I 'll come to ye, my lad!

I 'm O'er Young to Marry Yet

CHORUS

I 'm o'er young, I 'm o'er young,
    I 'm o'er young to marry yet!
I 'm o'er young, 't wad be a sin
    To tak me frae my mammie yet.

I

I am my mammie's ae bairn,
    Wi' unco folk I weary, Sir,
And lying in a man's bed,
    I 'm fley'd it make me eerie, Sir.

II

Hallowmass is come and gane,
    The nights are lang in winter, Sir,
And you an' I in ae bed—
    In trowth, I dare na venture, Sir!

III

Fu' loud and shrill the frosty wind
    Blaws thro' the leafless timmer, Sir,
But if ye come this gate again,
    I 'll aulder be gin simmer, Sir.

CHORUS

    I 'm o'er young, I 'm o'er young,
        I 'm o'er young to marry yet!
    I 'm o'er young, 't wad be a sin
        To tak me frae my mammie yet.

The Birks of Aberfeldie

CHORUS

        Bonie lassie, will ye go,
        Will ye go, will ye go?
        Bonie lassie, will ye go
            To the birks of Aberfeldie?

I

Now simmer blinks on flow'ry braes,
And o'er the crystal streamlets plays,
Come, let us spend the lightsome days
    In the birks of Aberfeldie!

II

The little birdies blythely sing,
While o'er their heads the hazels hing,
Or lightly flit on wanton wing
    In the birks of Aberfeldie.

III

The braes ascend like lofty wa's,
The foaming stream, deep-roaring, fa's
O'er hung with fragrant-spreading shaws,
    The birks of Aberfeldie.

IV

The hoary cliffs are crown'd wi' flowers,
White o'er the linns the burnie pours,
And, rising, weets wi' misty showers
     The birks of Aberfeldie.

V

Let Fortune's gifts at random flee,
They ne'er shall draw a wish frae me,
Supremely blest wi' love and thee
     In the birks of Aberfeldie.

CHORUS

     Bonie lassie, will ye go,
     Will ye go, will ye go?
     Bonie lassie, will ye go
          To the birks of Aberfeldie?

O'er the Water to Charlie

CHORUS

We 'll o'er the water, we 'll o'er the sea,
     We 'll o'er the water to Charlie!
Come weal, come woe, we 'll gather and go,
     And live and die wi' Charlie!

I

Come boat me o'er, come row me o'er,
     Come boat me o'er to Charlie!
I 'll gie John Ross another bawbee
     To boat me o'er to Charlie.

II

I lo'e weel my Charlie's name,
     Tho' some there be abhor him;
But O, to see Auld Nick gaun hame,
     And Charlie's faes before him!

III

I swear and vow by moon and stars
  And sun that shines so early,
If I had twenty thousand lives,
  I 'd die as aft for Charlie!

CHORUS

  We 'll o'er the water, we 'll o'er the sea,
    We 'll o'er the water to Charlie!
  Come weal, come woe, we 'll gather and go,
    And live and die wi' Charlie!

My Love, She 's But a Lassie Yet

CHORUS

    My love, she 's but a lassie yet,
    My love, she 's but a lassie yet!
  We 'll let her stand a year or twa,
    She 'll no be half sae saucy yet!

I

    I rue the day I sought her, O!
    I rue the day I sought her, O!
  Wha gets her need na say he 's woo'd,
    But he may say he has bought her, O.

II

    Come draw a drap o' the best o't yet,
    Come draw a drap o' the best o't yet!
  Gae seek for pleasure whare ye will,
    But here I never missed it yet.

III

    We 're a' dry wi' drinkin o't,
    We 're a' dry wi' drinkin o't!
  The minister kiss't the fiddler's wife—
    He could na preach for thinkin o't!

CHORUS

> My love, she 's but a lassie yet,
> My love, she 's but a lassie yet!
> We 'll let her stand a year or twa,
> She 'll no be half sae saucy yet!

The Silver Tassie

I

Go, fetch to me a pint o' wine,
    And fill it in a silver tassie,
That I may drink before I go
    A service to my bonie lassie!
The boat rocks at the pier o' Leith,
    Fu' loud the wind blaws frae the Ferry,
The ship rides by the Berwick-Law,
    And I maun leave my bonie Mary.

II

The trumpets sound, the banners fly,
    The glittering spears are rankèd ready,
The shouts o' war are heard afar,
    The battle closes deep and bloody.
It 's not the roar o' sea or shore
    Wad mak me langer wish to tarry,
Nor shouts o' war that 's heard afar:
    It 's leaving thee, my bonie Mary!

Of A' the Airts

I

Of a' the airts the wind can blaw
    I dearly like the west,
For there the bonie lassie lives,
    The lassie I lo'e best.

There wild woods grow, and rivers row,
    And monie a hill between,
But day and night my fancy's flight
    Is ever wi' my Jean.

II

I see her in the dewy flowers—
    I see her sweet and fair.
I hear her in the tunefu' birds—
    I hear her charm the air.
There 's not a bonie flower that springs
    By fountain, shaw, or green,
There 's not a bonie bird that sings,
    But minds me o' my Jean.

Whistle O'er the Lave o't

I

First when Maggie was my care,
Heav'n, I thought, was in her air;
Now we 're married, spier nae mair,
        But—whistle o'er the lave o't!
Meg was meek, and Meg was mild,
Sweet and harmless as a child:
Wiser men than me 's beguiled—
        Whistle o'er the lave o't!

II

How we live, my Meg and me,
How we love, and how we gree,
I care na by how few may see—
        Whistle o'er the lave o't!
Wha I wish were maggots' meat,
Dish'd up in her winding-sheet,
I could write (but Meg wad see 't)—
        Whistle o'er the lave o't!

My Heart 's in the Highlands

CHORUS

My heart 's in the Highlands, my heart is not here,
My heart 's in the Highlands a-chasing the deer,
A-chasing the wild deer and following the roe—
My heart 's in the Highlands, wherever I go!

I

Farewell to the Highlands, farewell to the North,
The birthplace of valour, the country of worth!
Wherever I wander, wherever I rove,
The hills of the Highlands for ever I love.

II

Farewell to the mountains high cover'd with snow,
Farewell to the straths and green valleys below,
Farewell to the forests and wild-hanging woods,
Farewell to the torrents and loud-pouring floods!

CHORUS

My heart 's in the Highlands, my heart is not here,
My heart 's in the Highlands a-chasing the deer,
A-chasing the wild deer and following the roe—
My heart 's in the Highlands, wherever I go!

John Anderson My Jo

I

John Anderson my jo, John,
   When we were first acquent,
Your locks were like the raven,
   Your bonie brow was brent;
But now your brow is beld, John,
   Your locks are like the snaw,
But blessings on your frosty pow,
   John Anderson my jo!

II

John Anderson my jo, John,
   We clamb the hill thegither,
And monie a cantie day, John,
   We 've had wi' ane anither;
Now we maun totter down, John,
   And hand in hand we 'll go,
And sleep thegither at the foot,
   John Anderson my jo!

Ca' the Yowes to the Knowes

CHORUS

Ca' the yowes to the knowes,
Ca' them where the heather grows,
Ca' them where the burnie rowes,
   My bonie dearie!

I

As I gaed down the water-side,
There I met my shepherd lad:
He row'd me sweetly in his plaid,
   And he ca'd me his dearie.

II

"Will ye gang down the water-side,
  And see the waves sae sweetly glide
Beneath the hazels spreading wide?
   The moon it shines fu' clearly."

III

"I was bred up in nae sic school,
  My shepherd lad, to play the fool,
An' a' the day to sit in dool,
   An' naebody to see me."

IV

"Ye sall get gowns and ribbons meet,
  Cauf-leather shoon upon your feet,
  And in my arms thou 'lt lie and sleep,
    An' ye sall be my dearie."

V

"If ye 'll but stand to what ye 've said,
  I 'se gang wi' you, my shepherd lad,
  And ye may row me in your plaid,
    And I sall be your dearie."

VI

"While waters wimple to the sea,
  While day blinks in the lift sae hie,
  Till clay-cauld death sall blin' my e'e,
    Ye sall be my dearie."

CHORUS

  Ca' the yowes to the knowes,
  Ca' them where the heather grows,
  Ca' them where the burnie rowes,
    My bonie dearie!

Willie Brew'd a Peck o' Maut

CHORUS

  We are na fou, we 're nae that fou,
    But just a drappie in our e'e!
  The cock may craw, the day may daw,
    And ay we 'll taste the barley-bree!

I

O, Willie brew'd a peck o' maut,
    And Rob and Allan cam to see.
Three blyther hearts that lee-lang night
    Ye wad na found in Christendie.

II

Here are we met three merry boys,
    Three merry boys I trow are we;
And monie a night we 've merry been,
    And monie mae we hope to be!

III

It is the moon, I ken her horn,
    That 's blinkin in the lift sae hie:
She shines sae bright to wyle us hame,
    But, by my sooth, she 'll wait a wee!

IV

Wha first shall rise to gang awa,
    A cuckold, coward loun is he!
Wha first beside his chair shall fa',
    He is the King amang us three!

CHORUS

We are na fou, we 're nae that fou,
    But just a drappie in our e'e!
The cock may craw, the day may daw,
    And ay we 'll taste the barley-bree!

Ae Fond Kiss

I

Ae fond kiss, and then we sever!
Ae farewell, and then forever!
Deep in heart-wrung tears I 'll pledge thee,
Warring sighs and groans I 'll wage thee.
Who shall say that Fortune grieves him,

While the star of hope she leaves him?
Me, nae cheerfu' twinkle lights me,
Dark despair around benights me.

II

I 'll ne'er blame my partial fancy:
Naething could resist my Nancy!
But to see her was to love her,
Love but her, and love for ever.
Had we never lov'd sae kindly,
Had we never lov'd sae blindly,
Never met—or never parted—
We had ne'er been broken-hearted.

III

Fare-the-weel, thou first and fairest!
Fare-the-weel, thou best and dearest!
Thine be ilka joy and treasure,
Peace, Enjoyment, Love and Pleasure!
Ae fond kiss, and then we sever!
Ae farewell, alas, for ever!
Deep in heart-wrung tears I 'll pledge thee,
Warring sighs and groans I 'll wage thee.

The Posie

I

O, luve will venture in where it daur na weel be seen!
O, luve will venture in, where wisdom ance hath been!
But I will doun yon river rove amang the wood sae green,
    And a' to pu' a posie to my ain dear May!

II

The primrose I will pu', the firstling o' the year,
And I will pu' the pink, the emblem o' my dear,
For she 's the pink o' womankind, and blooms without a peer—
    And a' to be a posie to my ain dear May!

III

I 'll pu' the budding rose when Phœbus peeps in view,
For it 's like a baumy kiss o' her sweet, bonie mou.
The hayacinth 's for constancy wi' its unchanging blue—
    And a' to be a posie to my ain dear May!

IV

The lily it is pure, and the lily it is fair,
And in her lovely bosom I 'll place the lily there.
The daisy 's for simplicity and unaffected air—
    And a' to be a posie to my ain dear May!

V

The hawthorn I will pu', wi' its locks o' siller gray,
Where, like an agèd man, it stands at break o' day;
But the songster's nest within the bush I winna tak away—
    And a' to be a posie to my ain dear May!

VI

The woodbine I will pu' when the e'ening star is near,
And the diamond draps o' dew shall be her een sae clear!
The violet 's for modesty, which weel she fa's to wear—
    And a' to be a posie to my ain dear May!

VII

I 'll tie the posie round wi' the silken band o' luve,
And I 'll place it in her breast, and I 'll swear by a' above,
That to my latest draught o' life the band shall ne'er remove,
    And this will be a posie to my ain dear May!

The Banks o' Doon

I

Ye banks and braes o' bonie Doon,
    How can ye bloom sae fresh and fair?
How can ye chant, ye little birds,
    And I sae weary fu' o' care!
Thou 'll break my heart, thou warbling bird,

That wantons thro' the flowering thorn!
Thou minds me o' departed joys,
    Departed never to return.

II

Aft hae I rov'd by bonie Doon
    To see the rose and woodbine twine,
And ilka bird sang o' its luve,
    And fondly sae did I o' mine.
Wi' lightsome heart I pu'd a rose,
    Fu' sweet upon its thorny tree!
And my fause luver staw my rose—
    But ah! he left the thorn wi' me.

Sweet Afton

I

Flow gently, sweet Afton, among thy green braes!
Flow gently, I 'll sing thee a song in thy praise!
My Mary 's asleep by thy murmuring stream—
Flow gently, sweet Afton, disturb not her dream!

II

Thou stock dove whose echo resounds thro' the glen,
Ye wild whistling blackbirds in yon thorny den,
Thou green-crested lapwing, thy screaming forbear—
I charge you, disturb not my slumbering fair!

III

How lofty, sweet Afton, thy neighbouring hills,
Far mark'd with the courses of clear, winding rills!
There daily I wander, as noon rises high,
My flocks and my Mary's sweet cot in my eye.

IV

How pleasant thy banks and green vallies below,
Where wild in the woodlands the primroses blow.

There oft, as mild Ev'ning weeps over the lea,
The sweet-scented birk shades my Mary and me.

V

Thy crystal stream, Afton, how lovely it glides,
And winds by the cot where my Mary resides!
How wanton thy waters her snowy feet lave,
As, gathering sweet flowerets, she stems thy clear wave!

VI

Flow gently, sweet Afton, among thy green braes!
Flow gently, sweet river, the theme of my lays!
My Mary 's asleep by thy murmuring stream—
Flow gently, sweet Afton, disturb not her dream!

The Deil 's Awa wi' th' Exciseman

CHORUS

    The Deil 's awa, the Deil 's awa,
        The Deil 's awa wi' th' Exciseman!
    He 's danc'd awa, he 's danc'd awa,
        He 's danc'd awa wi' th' Exciseman!

I

The Deil cam fiddlin thro' the town,
    And danc'd awa wi' th' Exciseman,
And ilka wife cries:—"Auld Mahoun,
    I wish you luck o' the prize, man!

II

"We 'll mak our maut, and we 'll brew our drink,
    We 'll laugh, sing, and rejoice, man,
And monie braw thanks to the meikle black Deil,
    That danc'd awa wi' th' Exciseman."

III

There 's threesome reels, there 's foursome reels,
    There 's hornpipes and strathspeys, man,
But the ae best dance e'er cam to the land
    Was *The Deil 's Awa wi' th' Exciseman.*

CHORUS

    The Deil 's awa, the Deil 's awa,
        The Deil 's awa wi' th' Exciseman!
    He 's danc'd awa, he 's danc'd awa,
        He 's danc'd awa wi' th' Exciseman!

A Red, Red Rose

I

    O, my luve is like a red, red rose,
        That 's newly sprung in June.
    O, my luve is like the melodie,
        That 's sweetly play'd in tune.

II

    As fair art thou, my bonie lass,
        So deep in luve am I,
    And I will luve thee still, my dear,
        Till a' the seas gang dry.

III

    Till a' the seas gang dry, my dear,
        And the rocks melt wi' the sun!
    And I will luve thee still, my dear,
        While the sands o' life shall run.

IV

    And fare thee weel, my only luve,
        And fare thee weel a while!
    And I will come again, my luve,
        Tho' it were ten thousand mile!

Auld Lang Syne

CHORUS

> For auld lang syne, my dear,
>   For auld lang syne,
> We 'll tak a cup o' kindness yet
>   For auld lang syne!

I

Should auld acquaintance be forgot,
    And never brought to mind?
Should auld acquaintance be forgot,
    And auld lang syne!

II

And surely ye 'll be your pint-stowp,
    And surely I 'll be mine,
And we 'll tak a cup o' kindness yet
    For auld lang syne!

III

We twa hae run about the braes,
    And pou'd the gowans fine,
But we 've wander'd monie a weary fit
    Sin' auld lang syne.

IV

We twa hae paidl'd in the burn
    Frae morning sun till dine,
But seas between us braid hae roar'd
    Sin' auld lang syne.

V

And there 's a hand, my trusty fiere,
    And gie 's a hand o' thine,
And we 'll tak a right guid-willie waught
    For auld lang syne!

CHORUS

> For auld lang syne, my dear,
>> For auld lang syne,
> We 'll tak a cup o' kindness yet
>> For auld lang syne!

Comin thro' the Rye

CHORUS

O, Jenny 's a' weet, poor body,
> Jenny 's seldom dry:
She draigl't a' her petticoatie,
> Comin thro' the rye!

I

> Comin thro' the rye, poor body,
>> Comin thro' the rye,
> She draigl't a' her petticoatie,
>> Comin thro' the rye!

II

> Gin a body meet a body
>> Comin thro' the rye,
> Gin a body kiss a body,
>> Need a body cry?

III

> Gin a body meet a body
>> Comin thro' the glen,
> Gin a body kiss a body,
>> Need the warld ken?

CHORUS

O, Jenny 's a' weet, poor body,
> Jenny 's seldom dry:
She draigl't a' her petticoatie,
> Comin thro' the rye!

Charlie He 's My Darling

CHORUS

> An' Charlie he 's my darling,
>> My darling, my darling,
> Charlie he 's my darling—
>> The Young Chevalier!

I

'T was on a Monday morning
> Right early in the year,
That Charlie came to our town—
> The Young Chevalier!

II

As he was walking up the street
> The city for to view,
O, there he spied a bonie lass
> The window looking thro'!

III

Sae light 's he jimpèd up the stair,
> And tirl'd at the pin;
And wha sae ready as hersel'
> To let the laddie in!

IV

He set his Jenny on his knee,
> All in his Highland dress;
For brawlie weel he kend the way
> To please a bonie lass.

O, Lay Thy Loof in Mine, Lass

CHORUS

> O, lay thy loof in mine, lass,
> In mine, lass, in mine, lass,

And swear on thy white hand, lass,
That thou wilt be my ain!

I

A slave to Love's unbounded sway,
He aft has wrought me meikle wae;
But now he is my deadly fae,
Unless thou be my ain.

II

There 's monie a lass has broke my rest,
That for a blink I hae lo'ed best;
But thou art queen within my breast,
For ever to remain.

CHORUS

O, lay thy loof in mine, lass,
In mine, lass, in mine, lass,
And swear on thy white hand, lass,
That thou wilt be my ain!

Open the Door to Me, O

I

O, open the door some pity to shew,
If love it may na be, O!
Tho' thou hast been false, I 'll ever prove true—
O, open the door to me, O!

II

Cauld is the blast upon my pale cheek,
But caulder thy love for me, O:
The frost, that freezes the life at my heart,
Is nought to my pains frae thee, O!

III

The wan moon sets behind the white wave,
And Time is setting with me, O:

False friends, false love, farewell! for mair
    I 'll ne'er trouble them nor thee, O!

IV

She has open'd the door, she has open'd it wide,
    She sees the pale corse on the plain, O,
"My true love!" she cried, and sank down by his side—
    Never to rise again, O!

Scots, Wha Hae

I

Scots, wha hae wi' Wallace bled,
Scots, wham Bruce has aften led,
Welcome to your gory bed
                Or to victorie!

II

Now 's the day, and now 's the hour:
See the front o' battle lour,
See approach proud Edward's power—
                Chains and slaverie!

III

Wha will be a traitor knave?
Wha can fill a coward's grave?
Wha sae base as be a slave?—
                Let him turn, and flee!

IV

Wha for Scotland's King and Law
Freedom's sword will strongly draw,
Freeman stand or freeman fa',
                Let him follow me!

V

By Oppression's woes and pains,
By your sons in servile chains,

We will drain our dearest veins
   But they shall be free!

VI

Lay the proud usurpers low!
Tyrants fall in every foe!
Liberty 's in every blow!
   Let us do, or die!

Highland Mary

I

Ye banks and braes and streams around
 The castle o' Montgomery,
Green be your woods, and fair your flowers,
 Your waters never drumlie!
There Summer first unfald her robes,
 And there the langest tarry!
For there I took the last fareweel
 O' my sweet Highland Mary!

II

How sweetly bloom'd the gay, green birk,
 How rich the hawthorn's blossom,
As underneath their fragrant shade
 I clasp'd her to my bosom!
The golden hours on angel wings
 Flew o'er me and my dearie:
For dear to me as light and life
 Was my sweet Highland Mary.

III

Wi' monie a vow and lock'd embrace
 Our parting was fu' tender;
And, pledging aft to meet again,
 We tore oursels asunder.
But O, fell Death's untimely frost,
 That nipt my flower sae early!

Now green 's the sod, and cauld 's the clay,
   That wraps my Highland Mary!

IV

O, pale, pale now, those rosy lips
   I aft hae kiss'd sae fondly;
And clos'd for ay, the sparkling glance
   That dwalt on me sae kindly;
And mouldering now in silent dust
   That heart that lo'ed me dearly!
But still within my bosom's core
   Shall live my Highland Mary.

There Was a Lad

CHORUS

     Robin was a rovin boy,
       Rantin, rovin, rantin, rovin,
     Robin was a rovin boy,
       Rantin, rovin Robin!

I

There was a lad was born in Kyle,
But whatna day o' whatna style,
I doubt it 's hardly worth the while
   To be sae nice wi' Robin.

II

Our monarch's hindmost year but ane
Was five and twenty days begun
'T was then a blast o' Janwar' win'
   Blew hansel in on Robin.

III

The gossip keekit in his loof,
Quo' scho:—"Wha lives will see the proof,
This waly boy will be nae coof:
   I think we 'll ca' him Robin.

IV

"He 'll hae misfortunes great an' sma',
But ay a heart aboon them a'.
He 'll be a credit till us a':
 We 'll a' be proud o' Robin!

V

"But sure as three times three mak nine,
I see by ilka score and line,
This chap will dearly like our kin',
 So leeze me on thee, Robin!

VI

"Guid faith," quo' scho, "I doubt you, stir,
Ye gar the lasses lie aspar;
But twenty fauts ye may hae waur—
 So blessins on thee, Robin!"

CHORUS

  Robin was a rovin boy,
   Rantin, rovin, rantin, rovin,
  Robin was a rovin boy,
   Rantin, rovin Robin!

O, Wert Thou in the Cauld Blast

I

O, wert thou in the cauld blast
 On yonder lea, on yonder lea,
My plaidie to the angry airt,
 I 'd shelter thee, I 'd shelter thee.
Or did Misfortune's bitter storms
 Around thee blaw, around thee blaw,
Thy bield should be my bosom,
 To share it a', to share it a'.

II

Or were I in the wildest waste,
    Sae black and bare, sae black and bare,
The desert were a Paradise,
    If thou wert there, if thou wert there.
Or were I monarch of the globe,
    Wi' thee to reign, wi' thee to reign,
The brightest jewel in my crown
    Wad be my queen, wad be my queen.

Glossary

A', all.
A-back, behind, away.
Aboon, above.
Abread, abroad.
Acquent, acquainted.
Ae, one.
Aff, off.
Aft, oft.
Aften, often.
Agley, askew.
Aiblins, ablins, may be, perhaps.
Ain, own.
Airn, iron.
Airt, direction.
Aits, oats.
A-jee, ajar.
Alake, alas.
Amaist, almost.
Amang, among.
Ance, once.
Ane, one.
Anither, another.
Aspar, aspread.
Auld, old.
Ava, at all, of all.
Awa, away.
Awnie, bearded.
Ay, aye, always.
Ayont, beyond.

Back-yett, back gate.
Bainie, banie, bony, big-boned.
Bairn, child.
Baith, both.
Bane, bone.
Barefit, barefooted.

Barley-brie or *-bree*, barley-liquor = ale or whisky.
Bauld, bold.
Baumy, balmy.
Bawbee, a halfpenny.
Baws'nt, white-streaked.
Bear, barley.
Beet, to feed, kindle, fan, add fuel to.
Beld, bald.
Belyve, by-and-by.
Ben, a parlor.
Ben, into the spence or parlor.
Beuk, a book: "devil's pictur'd beuks" = playing-cards.
Bicker, a wooden cup.
Bickering, hurrying.
Biel, bield, beild, a shelter, a sheltered spot.
Big, to build.
Biggin, a structure, a dwelling.
Bill, a bull.
Billie, fellow, comrade, brother.
Birk, the birch.
Birkie, a fellow (usually implies conceit).
Bit, nick of time.
Bizz, a flurry.
Bizz, to buzz.
Black-bonnet, the elder.
Blastet, blastit, blasted (used in contempt and equivalent to *damn'd*).
Blastie, a blasted (*i.e.* damn'd) creature.
Blate, modest, bashful, shy.
Blather, blether, bladder.
Blaw, to blow.

Bleeze, to blaze.
Blellum, a babbler.
Blether, to talk nonsense.
Blinkers, spies.
Bluid, blood.
Boddle, a farthing (properly two pennies Scots, or one sixth of an English penny).
Body, bodie, a person, a creature.
Bogle, a bogie, a hobgoblin.
Bonie, bonnie, pretty, beautiful.
Boord, board, surface.
Boortrees, the shrub-elder.
Bore, a chink, a small hole, an opening.
Bowse, drink, booze.
Brae, a small hill, the slope of a hill.
Braid, broad.
Braid-claith, broad-cloth.
Brak, brake, broke.
Brash, short illness.
Brattle, a spurt, a scamper.
Braw, gaily dressed, fine, handsome.
Brawlie, finely, perfectly, heartily.
Breeks, breeches.
Brent, brand.
Brent, straight, steep (*i.e.* not sloping from baldness).
Brig, bridge.
Brither, brother.
Brock, a badger.
Brogue, a trick.
Brunstane, brimstone.
Buirdly, stout, stalwart.
Bum, to hum.
Bum-clock, a humming beetle.
Burdie, dim. of *bird* or *burd* (a lady), a maiden.
Burn, a rivulet.
Burnewin, the blacksmith (*i.e.* burn the wind).
But, butt, in the kitchen (*i.e.* the outer apartment), "butt the house" = in the kitchen.
Byke, bike, a bees' nest, a hive.

Ca', to call, to drive (*e.g.* cattle).
Caff, chaff.
Caller, cool, refreshing.

Cam, came.
Canie, cannie, gentle, tractable, quiet, prudent, careful.
Canna, cannot.
Cannilie, cannily, quietly, prudently, cautiously.
Cantie, cheerful, lively, jolly, merry.
Cantraip, magic, witching.
Carlin, carline, a middle-aged, or old woman, a beldam, a witch.
Cartes, playing cards.
Cauk, chalk: "o' cauk and keel" = in chalk and ruddle.
Cauld, cold.
Caup, a wooden drinking-vessel (*i.e.* cup).
Chamer, chaumer, chamber.
Change-house, tavern.
Chapman, a pedlar.
Chaup, chap, a stroke, a blow.
Chiel, chield (child) a fellow, a young fellow (indicates approval).
Chows, chews.
Claes, claise, clothes.
Clap, the clapper of a mill.
Claucht, claught, clutched, seized.
Cleek, to take hold.
Clinkin, with a smart motion.
Clinkum, Clinkumbell, the beadle, the bellman.
Cloot, a cloven hoof, one of the divisions of a cloven hoof.
Clootie, Cloots, Hoofie, Hoofs (a nickname of the devil).
Coft, bought.
Cog, a wooden drinking-vessel.
Cood, cud.
Coof, dolt.
Coost (cast), looped, threw off.
Cootie, a wooden dish.
Core, corps.
Cot, cottage.
Cot-folk, Cotters, cottagers, peasants.
Cour, to lower.
Crack, a tale, talk.
Crack, to converse, to chat, to talk.
Craig, the throat.
Cranks, creakings.

Cranreuch, hoar-frost, rime.
Craw, crow.
Creeshie, greasy.
Croon, to boom, hum.
Croose, crouse, cocksure, lively, jolly.
Crouse, cheerfully.
Crowdie-time, porridge-time (*i.e.* breakfast-time).
Crowlin, crawling.
Crummock, cummock, a cudgel, a crooked staff.
Crump, crisp.
Cuif, coof, a dull, spiritless fellow, a dolt, a ninny.
Curchie, a curtsy.
Cutty, short.

Daffin, larking, fun.
Dails, deals, planks.
Daimen icker, an occasional ear of corn.
Darg, daurk, labor, task, a day's labor.
Daur, dare.
Daut, dawte, to fondle, to pet.
Daw, to dawn.
Dawds, lumps, large portions.
Deil, deevil, devil.
Deil-haet, nothing (the devil have it).
Dight, to winnow.
Dine, dinner.
Ding, to beat, to surpass.
Dinna, do not.
Dirl, to vibrate, to ring.
Diz'n, dizzen, dozen.
Doited, muddled, stupid, bewildered.
Donsie, unlucky.
Dool, woe, sorrow.
Douce, douse, sedate, sober, serious, prudent.
Doun, down.
Dow, dowe, am (is or are) able, can.
Doylt, stupid, stupefied.
Doytin, doddering.
Draigl't, draggled.
Drap, drop.
Droddum, the breech.
Drouthy, thirsty.
Druken, drucken, drunken.
Drumlie, muddy, turbid.

Dub, a puddle.
Duddie, ragged.
Duddies, dim. of *duds*, rags.
Duds, rags, clothes.
Dwalt, dwelt.
Dyke, a fence (of stone or turf), a wall.

E'e, eye.
Een, eyes.
E'en, evening.
Eerie, apprehensive, inspiring ghostly fear.
Eldritch, horrible, unearthly, haunted, fearsome.
Eneugh, enough.
Erse, Gaelic.
Ettle, aim.
Ev'n down, downright, positive.
Eydent, diligent.

Fa', a fall, a lot, a portion.
Fa', to fall, to receive as one's portion.
Fae, foe.
Faem, foam.
Fain, fond, glad.
Fairin, a present from a fair.
Fand, found.
Farls, small, thin oat-cakes.
Fash, to trouble, to bother, to worry.
Fatt'rils, ribbon ends.
Faulding, folding, sheep-folding.
Faut, fault.
Fawsont, seemly, decent.
Fecht, to fight.
Feck, the bulk, the most part.
Fell, keen, cruel, dreadful, deadly, pungent.
Ferlie, ferly, a wonder (used contemptuously).
Ferlie, to marvel.
Fidge, to fidget, to wriggle.
Fient a, not a: "the fient a" = nothing of a.
Fient haet o', not one of.
Fier, fiere, comrade.
Fit, foot.
Flainin, flannen, flannel.
Flee, to fly.

Fley, to scare.
Flichterin', fluttering.
Fodgel, dumpy.
Foggage, meadow grass.
Forby, forbye, besides.
Fou, fow, full (usually in the sense of drunk).
Foughten, troubled.
Fouth, fulness, abundance.
Frae, from.
Freath, to froth.
Fu', full.
Fur, furr, a furrow.
Furm, a wooden form.
Fyke, fuss.
Fyle, to defile, to foul, to soil.

Gab, the mouth, the jaw.
Gaen, gane, gone.
Gaets, ways, manners.
Gang, to go, to walk.
Gar, to cause, to make, to compel.
Gash, wise, sagacious, self-complacent (implying prudence and prosperity).
Gat, got.
Gate, way, road, manner.
Gaun, going.
Gawsie, gaucie, buxom, buxom and jolly.
Gear, money, wealth, goods, stuff.
Geordie, dim. of *George*; hence a guinea, bearing the image and superscription of King George.
Ghaist, ghost.
Gie, to give.
Gin, if, should, whether.
Gin, against, by.
Gizz, wig.
Glaikit, foolish, thoughtless, giddy.
Gleg, sharp, quick, keen.
Gloamin, gloaming, twilight, dusk.
Glow'r, a stare, to stare.
Glunch, a frown, a sour look.
Gooms, gums.
Gowan, the wild daisy.
Grain, groan.
Graith, implements, tools, gear, attire, garb.

Grannie, Graunie, grandmother.
Gree, to agree.
Greet, to weep.
Grip, gripe.
Grozet, a gooseberry.
Gruntle, the snout, the face.
Grushie, growing.
Gude, God.
Guid, gude, good.
Guid-willie, gude-willie, hearty, full of goodwill.
Gullie, gully, a large knife.
Gusty, tasty.

Ha', hall.
Ha' folk, the servants.
Hae, have.
Haffet, hauffet, the temple, the side of the head.
Hafflins, half, partly.
Hain, to spare, to save.
Haith, faith! (a petty oath).
Hal', hald, holding, abiding-place.
Hale, hail, whole, healthy.
Hallan, a partition between the door of a cottage and the fireplace.
Hallowmass, All Saints' Day (1st November).
Haly, holy.
Hame, home.
Hangie, hangman (nickname of the devil).
Hansel, the first gift.
Happer, hopper (of a mill).
Hap-step-an'-lowp, hop-step-and-leap (an important item in Scots athletic gatherings, but here used metaphorically of course).
Harn, coarse cloth (cloth spun of "hards," *i.e.* coarse flax).
Hash, an oaf, a dunderhead.
Haud, to hold, to keep.
Haughs, low-lying rich lands, valleys.
Havins, good manners, good conduct.
Hawkie, a white-faced cow, a cow.
Hech, ah!
Het, hot.
Heugh, a crag, a steep bank.

Hie, high.
Himsel, himself.
Hing, to hang.
Hirple, to limp, to hobble.
Histie, bare.
Hizzie, a hussy, a wench, a young woman.
Hoast, a cough.
Hoddin, the motion of a sage countryman riding on a cart horse.
Hoord, hoard.
Hornie, the devil.
Hotch'd, hitched, jerked (the action of a bagpiper's arm).
Houghmagandie, fornication.
Howdie, howdy, a midwife.
Howk, to dig out.
Howlet, houlet, an owl.
Hunder, a hundred.
Hurdies, the loins, the crupper.

Ilk, ilka, each, every.
Indentin, indenturing.
Ingle, the fire, the fireplace.
Ither, other, each other, one another.

Jad, a jade.
Jauk, to trifle, to dally.
Jimp, jump.
Jink, to frisk, to sport, to move nimbly.
Jo, a sweetheart.
Jocteleg, a jack-knife.
Jow, a verb that includes both the swinging motion and pealing sound of a large bell.

Kail, kale, the colewort (also cabbage).
Kain, kane, rents in kind.
Kebbuck, a cheese.
Keek, to look, to peep, to glance.
Kelpies, river-demons (usually shaped as horses).
Ken, to know.
Kennin, a very little (merely as much as can be perceived).
Kiaugh, cark, anxiety.
Kirk, church.
Kirn, a churn.

Kirn, harvest-home.
Kittle, to tickle.
Knowe, a knoll, a hillock.
Kye, kine, cows.

Lade, a load.
Lag, slow.
Laird, landowner (the lord of houses or lands).
Laith, loath, loth.
Laithfu', (loathful) sheepish.
Lallans, Scots Lowland vernacular.
Lane, lone.
Lang, long.
Lang-kail, coleworts not cut or chopped.
Lang syne, long since, long ago.
Lap, leapt.
Lave, the rest, the remainder, the others.
Laverock, lav'rock, the lark.
Lear, lore, learning.
Lee-lang, live-long.
Leeze me on (from *leis me* = dear is to me), how well I love, blessings on, commend me to.
Leuk, look.
Lift, the sky.
Lightly, to disparage.
Limmer, a jade, a mistress.
Link, to trip or dance with activity, to trip along.
Linn, lin, a waterfall.
Lint, flax.
Loan, a lane, a field-path, the private road to a farm or house.
Lo'ed, loved.
Loof, the palm of the hand.
Loon, loun, lown, a clown, a rascal.
Lough, a loch, a lake.
Loup, lowp, to leap.
Lowin, lowing, flaming, burning.
Lowse, louse, to loose, to untie.
Lug, the ear.
Lugget, having a handle.
Lume, a utensil.
Lunardi, a balloon-bonnet (named after Lunardi, a famous balloonist).

Lunches, full portions.
Luntin, smoking.
Lyart, gray.

Mahoun, a name for the devil.
Mailie, Molly.
Mair, more.
Maist, most.
Maist, almost.
Mak, make.
'*Mang*, among.
Manteele, a mantle.
Maun, must.
Maut, malt.
Meikle, *mickle*, *muckle*, much, great.
Melder, the quantity of corn sent to be ground.
Mell, to meddle, to be intimate, to mix.
Melvie, to dust with meal.
Men', to mend.
Menseless, unmannerly.
Messin, a little dog, a cur.
Mim, prim, affectedly meek.
Misca', to miscall, to abuse.
Mither, mother.
Monie, many.
Moop, to nibble.
Mou', the mouth.
Moudieworts, moles.
Muckle, much.

Na, *nae*, no, not.
Naething, *naithing*, nothing.
Naig, a nag.
Nane, none.
Nappy, strong ale.
Neebor, *neibor*, neighbour.
Negleckit, neglected.
Neive, *nieve*, the fist.
Neuk, *newk*, a nook, a corner.
Nick (*Auld*), *Nickie-ben*, a name of the devil.
Nick, to sever, to cut, to cut down.
Nick-nackets, knicknacks, curiosities.
Niest, next.
Niffer, exchange.
Nowt, *nowte* (Engl. *neat*), cattle.

O', of.
Onie, any.
Owre, over, too.

Pack an' thick, confidential.
Paidle, to paddle, to wade.
Painch, the paunch.
Pang, to cram.
Parritch, porridge.
Parritch-pats, porridge-pots.
Pattle, *pettle*, a plough-staff.
Pechan, the stomach.
Penny wheep, small beer.
Philibeg, the Highlander's kilt.
Pit, put.
Plack, four pennies Scots (but only the third of an English penny).
Plackless, penniless.
Plaister, plaster.
Pleugh, *plew*, a plough.
Poind, to seize, to distrain, to impound.
Poortith, poverty.
Pou, to pull.
Pow, the poll, the head.
Prent, print.
Propone, propose.
Pu', pull.
Pun', *pund*, pound.
Pussie, a hare.
Pyles, grains.

Quat, quit, quitted.
Quean, a young woman, a lass.
Quo', *quod*, quoth.

Raible, to gabble.
Rair, to roar.
Rants, merry meetings, sprees.
Rape, rope.
Rash, a rush.
Rash-buss, a clump of rushes.
Raw, a row.
Ream, foam.
Reave, to rob.
Rede, counsel.
Reek, to smoke.
Reekit, smoked, smoky.
Reestit, singed.

Rig, a ridge (of land).
Riggin, a ridge (of a house), a roof.
Rigwoodie, ancient, lean.
Rin, to run.
Ripp, a handful of corn from the sheaf.
Rive, to split, to cleave, to rend, to tear.
Row, rowe, to roll, flow.
Rowte, to low, to bellow.
Rowth, routh, plenty, a store.
Rozet, rosin.
Run-deils, downright devils.
Runkl'd, wrinkled.

Sae, so.
Sair, sore, hard, severe, strong.
Sall, shall.
Sang, song.
Sark, a shirt, a shift.
Saul, soul.
Saunt, saint.
Saut-backets, saltboxes.
Sax, six.
Scaud, to scald.
Scaul, scold.
Scaur, scary, timid.
Scho, she.
Screed, a rip, a rent.
Scrievin, moving swiftly.
Shaw, a wood.
Sheugh, a ditch, a furrow.
Shog, a shake.
Shool, a shovel.
Shoon, shoes.
Sic, such.
Siller, silver, money in general, wealth.
Simmer, summer.
Sin', since.
Skellum, a good-for-nothing.
Skelp, to spank, to slap, to strike, to hasten, to move quickly.
Skirl, to cry or sound shrilly, to squeal, to squall.
Sklent, to slant, to squint.
Slae, the sloe.
Slap, a breach in a fence, an opening.
Sleekit, sleek.
Sma', small.

Smeddum, a powder.
Smiddie, smithy.
Smoor'd, smothered.
Smoutie, smutty.
Smytrie, a large collection of small individuals, a litter.
Snakin, sneering.
Snash, abuse.
Snaw, snow.
Sneeshin mill, a snuff-box.
Snell, bitter, biting.
Snick-drawing, scheming.
Snowkit, snuffed (expressive of the sound made by the dog's nose).
Sodger, soger, a soldier.
Sonsie, sonsy, pleasant, good-natured, jolly.
Souple, supple, flexible.
Souter, cobbler, a shoemaker.
Sowther, to solder.
Spairge, to splash.
Spak, spoke.
Spean, to wean.
Speel, to climb.
Speer, spier, to ask.
Splore, a frolic, a carousal.
Sprattle, to scramble.
Spunkie, a will-o'-the-wisp, a jack-o'-lantern.
Spurtle, a stick used for stirring porridge, etc.: "spurtle-blade" (used humorously of a sword).
Squattle, to squat, to settle.
Stacher, to stagger, to totter.
Stan', stand.
Stane, stone.
Startle, to course.
Staun', stand.
Stechin, cramming, stuffing.
Steek, a stitch.
Steer, to rouse, to stir.
Stell, a still.
Stents, assessments, dues, taxes.
Stibble, stubble.
Stoor, hoarse.
Stoure, dust.
Strang, strong.
Strath, valley.

Straught, straight.
Stroan't, pissed.
Strunt, to strut.
Studdie, an anvil.
Sturt, worry, trouble.
Sucker, sugar.
Sugh, sough, a sough, a moan, a sound as of the wind, a sigh.
Swaird, the sward.
Swankies, strapping fellows.
Swat, sweated.
Swatch, a sample.
Swats, new ale.
Swith, haste! off and away!
Syne, since, then, ago.

Tacket, a hob-nail.
Taen, taken.
Tak, to take.
Tapsalteerie, topsy-turvy.
Tassie, a cup.
Tauld, told.
Tawted, matted, with matted hair.
Teats, small quantities.
Tent, to tend, to heed, to observe.
Tentie, watchful, careful, heedful.
Tentless, careless, heedless.
Thack, thatch: "thack and rape" = the covering of a house, and therefore used as a simile for home necessities.
Thae, those.
Thegither, together.
Thir, these.
Thole, to endure, to suffer.
Thowe, thaw.
Thrang, crowded, busy.
Thrave, twenty-four sheaves of corn.
Timmer, timber.
Tinkler, a tinker.
Tint, lost.
Tippenny, two-penny ale.
Tirl, to strip, to uncover, to unroof, to rattle.
Tither, the other.
Tittlin, whispering.
Tod, the fox.
Toop, tip, a tup, a ram.

Tousie, shaggy.
Tow, flax, a rope.
Towmond, towmont, a twelve-month.
Toy, flapped cap of lower-class women.
Trashtrie, small trash.
Trowth, truth, In truth!
Twa, two.
Twal, twelve.
Twalpennie worth = a penny worth (sterling).
Twin, twine, to deprive, to rob.
Tyke, a dog.

Unco, remarkably, uncommonly, very.
Unco, strange.
Uncos, strange things, wonders, news.
Unfald, unfold.
Unkend, unknown.

Vauntie, vain, proud.
Vera, very.

Wa', waw, a wall.
Wabster, a weaver.
Wad, would, would have.
Wae, woeful, sorrowful (also used sarcastically).
Waesucks, alas!
Wae worth, woe befall.
Wale, choice.
Walie, waly, wawlie, ample, large, robust.
Wame, the belly.
Wanrestfu', restless.
Wark, work.
Warl'y, warldly, worldly.
Warsle, warstle, wrestle.
Warst, worst.
Wastrie, waste.
Water-fit, water-foot (the river's mouth).
Waught, a deep draught.
Wauken, to waken.
Waur, worse.
Wean, (wee one) a child.
Weanies, babies.
Weason, the weasand, the windpipe.
Wee, little.
Weel, well.

Weet, wet.

We 'se, we shall, we will.

Wha, who.

Whae'er, whoever.

Whalpit, whelped.

Wham, whom.

Whang, a large slice.

Whar, whare, whaur, where.

Wha 's, whase, whose.

Whatna, what, what kind of, (partly in contempt).

Whun-stane, whinstone, hard rock.

Whyles, sometimes, now and then.

Wi', with.

Wimple, to meander.

Winna, will not.

Winnock-bunker, window seat.

Wist, knew.

Wonner, a wonder, a marvel (sometimes used contemptuously).

Woo', wool.

Wrang, wrong.

Wud, mad, angry, raging.

Wyliecoat, undervest.

Wyte, to blame, to reproach.

Yard, a garden, a stackyard.

Yell, dry (milkless).

Yestreen, last night.

Yill, ale.

'Yont, beyond.

Yowe, ewe.

Alphabetical List of Titles

Alphabetical List of First Lines

[The first lines of choruses to songs are included]